WRITERS AND THEIR WORK
ISOBEL ARMSTRONG
General Editor

SIR PHILIP SIDNEY
AND THE SIDNEY CIRCLE

SIR PHILIP SIDNEY
AND THE SIDNEY CIRCLE

Matthew Woodcock

For my mother

© Copyright 2010 by Matthew Woodcock

First published in 2010 by Northcote House Publishers Ltd,
Horndon, Tavistock, Devon, PL19 9NQ, United Kingdom.
Tel: +44 (0) 1822 810066 Fax: +44 (0) 1822 810034.

All rights reserved. No part of this work may be reproduced or stored in an information retrieval system (other than short extracts for the purposes of review) without the express permission of the Publishers given in writing.

British Library Cataloguing-in-Publication Data
A catalogue record for this book is available from the British Library

ISBN 978-0-7463-1192-9 hardcover
ISBN 978-0-7463-1197-4 paperback
Typeset by PDQ Typesetting, Newcastle-under-Lyme
Printed and bound in the United Kingdom

Contents

Preface vi
Acknowledgements viii
Biographical Outline ix
Abbreviations xii
Note on the Texts xiii
1 The Courtly Performer 1
2 Arcadian Toys 18
3 Theory and Practice 36
4 *Astrophil and Stella* 49
5 Refashionings 63
6 The Sidney Circle 81
Notes 104
Select Bibliography 108
Index 119

Preface

Critical accounts of Sidney's life and writings frequently begin by listing numerous different roles that could be used to describe him: courtier, poet, patron, diplomat, soldier, humanist correspondent. No single term adequately embraces the multifaceted nature of his short yet complex life. Equally there are many different stories that can be told about Sidney, fashioning him variously as a model for his contemporaries of chivalric and courtly conduct, as an innovative literary craftsman and theorist, as the great hope of European militant Protestantism, or as the victim of Elizabeth's vacillatory domestic and foreign policy whose 'great expectations' of advancement were frustrated repeatedly. Sidney himself is often complicit in the creation of such stories, particularly those relating to his dashed hopes and obstructed ambitions in love and politics. Sidney's early death aged thirty-one, after being wounded at Zutphen in the Netherlands, initiates the myth-formation that often follows the premature death of a popular public figure. The creation of a Sidney 'myth' is another form of story-telling, but one in which what Sidney represents, and what he could or should have done had he lived, are just as significant – if not more so – than what he actually he did when alive. This book therefore attempts to address both the man and the myth, and remain sensitive to successive fashionings and refashionings of Sidney undertaken, not only by the writer himself, but by his closest contemporaries who play a significant role in shaping his posthumous reputation.

This book offers a structured introduction to Sidney's major writings through examining the relationship between the writer and his conception of his works' function. It would be misleading, however, to view Sidney wholly as a literary figure whose work can be divorced from his wider role as courtier and statesman.

Informed by the direction of Sidney scholarship of the last twenty-five years the present study also addresses the political and historical context of the writer's works and the complexity of his conception of what may (and should) be achieved in the public sphere through rhetoric and poetics. I therefore also discuss Sidney's writings in relation to his individual construction of personal identity, his cultural milieu and associated coterie and patronage networks, and his active response to the politics of continental Europe and the Elizabethan court. This book also discusses the so-called 'Sidney Circle', an expedient term used hereafter for those who were directly engaged in circulating Sidney's writings in manuscript, whose own literary output was influenced by Sidney, or who were involved in preparing Sidney's works for publication after his death and instrumental in perpetuating and protecting his literary identity and reputation. They are identified here as Philip's sister Mary, Countess of Pembroke, his friend Fulke Greville, his brother Robert Sidney and niece Lady Mary Wroth. Although loosely chronological in organization (recognizing the difficulties with precisely dating the production and revision of Sidney's works), this book is not a literary biography. Those interested in a more detailed survey of Sidney's life and the other stories that could be told regarding his diplomatic missions, links with continental humanists or interests in colonial ventures, are directed in the first instance to the biographical titles listed in the Bibliography.

Acknowledgements

My thanks go to Matthew Hansen, Andrew King, Matthew Steggle and Tom Rutledge for commenting on drafts of this book; and to Isobel Armstrong, Brian Hulme and Althea Stewart for making this project possible.

Biographical Outline

1554	Philip Sidney born (30 November). Fulke Greville born (3 October).
1561	Mary Sidney born (27 October).
1563	Robert Sidney born (19 November).
1564	Sidney and Greville enrolled at Shrewsbury School.
1568	Sidney enters Christ Church, Oxford. Greville enters Jesus College, Cambridge.
1572	Sidney visits France, witnesses St Bartholomew's Day Massacre (24 August) and begins his tour of continental Europe.
1575	Returns from Europe. Attends Leicester's entertainment for Queen Elizabeth at Kenilworth. Robert enters Christ Church, Oxford.
1576	Sidney visits his father in Ireland. Granted the ceremonial post of Cupbearer to Elizabeth. Greville begins his *Caelica* poems.
1577	Sidney and Greville sent on an embassy to Emperor Rudolf II in Prague. Sidney composes a pastoral dialogue for presentation at Wilton and may have started the *Old Arcadia*. Mary marries the Earl of Pembroke.
1578	Sidney writes *The Lady of May* for the entertainment at Wanstead.
1579	Sidney's tennis court quarrel with the Earl of Oxford. Writes a letter to Queen Elizabeth opposing the proposed Anjou match.
1580	*Old Arcadia* probably completed. May have begun *The Defence of Poesy*.
1581	Penelope Devereux marries Lord Rich. Sidney becomes Member of Parliament. He participates in the *Four Foster*

	Children of Desire tournament (with Greville) and starts his sonnet sequence *Astrophil and Stella*.
1582	Sidney escorts Anjou to Antwerp.
1583	Sidney knighted by proxy for Johann Casimir. Marries Frances Walsingham (21 September). May have started to revise the *Arcadia*.
1584	Sidney assigned to (aborted) diplomatic mission to France. Writes the *Defence of Leicester*. Robert marries heiress Barbara Gamage.
1585	In the early part of the year Sidney possibly began translations of the Psalms and works by de Mornay and du Bartas. Made Master of Ordnance (July). Attempts to join Sir Francis Drake's expedition to West Indies but is prevented by Elizabeth. Appointed governor of Flushing in the Netherlands (November). Robert accompanies brother Philip to Flushing.
1586	Sidney's father and mother, Sir Henry Sidney and Lady Mary Sidney, die. Sidney wounded at Zutphen (22 September); dies at Arnhem on 17 October.
1587	Sidney's funeral at St Paul's, London (16 February). Arthur Golding's completion of Sidney's translation of de Mornay published. Robert's eldest daughter Mary (later Lady Mary Wroth) born (18 October).
1589	Robert made governor of Flushing (he would retain the post until 1616).
1590	Greville publishes revised version of the *Arcadia*.
1591	First publication of *Astrophil and Stella*.
1592	Mary publishes her translations of works by de Mornay and Robert Garnier.
1593	Mary publishes the 'composite' *Arcadia* (books 1–3 of the *New* and 3–5 of the *Old*).
1595	Publication of *The Defence of Poesy* and the pirated edition, *An Apology for Poetry*.
1598	Publication of first 'collected works' of Sidney. Greville made Treasurer of the Navy.
1599	Mary completes her brother's unfinished translation of the Psalms. Greville begins choruses that become the *Treatise of Monarchy*.
1600	Mary translates Petrarch's *Triumph of Death*.
1601	Greville's *Letter to an Honourable Lady* completed. He also completes the revised *Alaham*. Earl of Pembroke dies.

	BIOGRAPHICAL OUTLINE
1603	Death of Elizabeth I; accession of James I.
1604	Robert's daughter Mary marries Sir Robert Wroth.
1605	Robert made Viscount De L'Isle.
1609	Pirated edition of *Mustapha* published.
1612	Greville completes the first version of the *Life of Sidney*.
1614	Greville made a privy councillor. Revision of the *Life of Sidney* completed.
1618	Robert made Earl of Leicester.
1619	Transcription of Warwick Castle manuscripts of Greville's works begins.
1621	Mary dies from smallpox (25 September). Greville made first Baron Brooke. He may have begun his *Treatise of Religion* and composed the last *Caelica* poems around this time. First part of Lady Mary Wroth's *The Countess of Montgomery's Urania* published.
1626	Robert dies (13 July).
1628	Greville fatally wounded by his servant; dies 30 September.
1633	Publication of Greville's *Certain Learned Works* collection.
1652	Publication of the *Life of Sidney*. According to a 1668 Chancery document Lady Mary Wroth dies in either 1651 or 1653.
1670	Greville's *Remains* (the treatises on monarchy and religion) published.

For a more detailed biographical overview of the Sidney family, consult Michael G. Brennan and Noel J. Kinnamon, *A Sidney Chronology, 1554–1654* (Basingstoke: Palgrave Macmillan, 2003).

Abbreviations

The following abbreviations are used in the main text:

Croft   *The Poems of Robert Sidney*, ed. P. J. Croft (Oxford: Clarendon Press, 1984).

Gouws   *The Prose Works of Fulke Greville*, ed. John Gouws (Oxford: Clarendon Press, 1986).

Gunn   *Selected Poems of Fulke Greville*, ed. Thom Gunn (London: Faber, 1968); for all quotations from *Caelica*.

Hannay   *The Collected Works of Mary Sidney Herbert, Countess of Pembroke*, ed. Margaret P. Hannay, Noel J. Kinnamon and Michael G. Brennan (2 vols; Oxford: Clarendon Press, 1998).

MP   *Miscellaneous Prose of Sir Philip Sidney*, ed. Katherine Duncan-Jones and Jan van Dorsten (Oxford: Clarendon Press, 1973); for the *Defence of Leicester*, 'Discourse on Irish Affairs' and *Letter to the Queen*.

MW   *Sir Philip Sidney: The Major Works*, ed. Katherine Duncan-Jones (2nd edn; Oxford: Oxford University Press, 2002); for all quotations from the Wilton dialogue, *The Lady of May*, *The Defence of Poesy*, *Astrophil and Stella*, *Certain Sonnets* and *Four Foster Children of Desire*.

NA   *The Countess of Pembroke's Arcadia* (the *New Arcadia*), ed. Maurice Evans (Harmondsworth: Penguin, 1977).

OA   *The Old Arcadia*, ed. Katherine Duncan-Jones (Oxford: Oxford University Press, 1985).

Roberts   *The Poems of Lady Mary Wroth*, ed. Josephine A. Roberts (Baton Rouge: Louisiana State University Press, 1983).

Wilkes   *The Remains, Being Poems of Monarchy and Religion*, ed. G. A. Wilkes (London: Oxford University Press, 1965).

Note on the Texts

There are several different versions of Sidney's *Arcadia*, the nomenclature for which requires clarification. First there is the five-book *Old Arcadia* that was completed in 1580 and circulated in manuscript during Sidney's lifetime and after. This version was lost until 1907 and first published in 1926. Nine manuscript copies are now known. Sidney began to revise the *Old Arcadia* in 1583–4 and reworked two books and part of the third before his death in 1586. This fragmented version was published in 1590 under the auspices of Fulke Greville, with each book divided into separate chapters, and is commonly referred to as the *New Arcadia* or *The Countess of Pembroke's Arcadia*. Greville also rearranged the sets of eclogues between each book. In 1593 Sidney's sister Mary published the *New Arcadia* together with books 3 to 5 of the old version to form a composite *Arcadia* never envisaged by Sidney. In 1621 Sir William Alexander wrote a bridging passage connecting the revised version with the original conclusion. It is this composite *Arcadia* that was read and celebrated for over three hundred years.

1

The Courtly Performer

We should begin by re-examining one of the most enduring images of Sir Philip Sidney: that he is the embodiment of the perfect Elizabethan courtier. This is not an unreasonable starting point given that many of his contemporaries made similar observations. Gabriel Harvey and Thomas Nashe agreed that Sidney stood out from their peers as an exemplar of the ideal courtier as characterized in Baldassare Castiglione's highly influential *Book of the Courtier* (1528). Sir Henry Sidney instructed Philip's younger brother Robert to 'imitate his virtues, studies, and actions', claiming (with obvious bias) that 'he is a rare ornament of this age, the very formula that all well-disposed young gentleman of our court do form also their manners and life by ... he hath the most rare virtues that ever I found in any man'.[1] The Elizabethan court has a dominant influence on Sidney's political career – or at least his ambitions for such a career – and on his writings. But what were Sidney's 'courtly' credentials? Indeed, what does it actually mean to be a 'courtier'? How useful is it to describe Sidney as a courtly poet, particularly given that much of his literary output, upon which his present fame largely rests, was produced when he was away from court?

If one were to construct the ideal c.v. or résumé for an aspiring Renaissance courtier it would be hard to find somebody with better qualifications and experience to draw on than the young Philip Sidney. For a start he had impeccable family connections. His father Sir Henry was a counsellor and favourite of Edward VI. In the summer of 1554, just before Philip was born, Sir Henry was sent to escort King Philip II of Spain to England to marry Mary I, and later invited the king to be his new-born son's godfather. With great irony, given the focus of

Sidney's political energies later in life, Philip was named after the Spanish monarch. Sir Henry continued to serve under Mary and Elizabeth, and was appointed Lord President of Wales in 1560 and Lord Deputy Governor of Ireland in 1565. As Lord Deputy, Sir Henry was Elizabeth's supreme representative in Ireland, and the Latin title of his post 'Pro-rex' (Viceroy) led many continental observers to regard him as a quasi-royal figure. Sir Henry had also married well: Philip's mother, Lady Mary Sidney, was the daughter of the Duke of Northampton and sister of Robert Dudley, the Earl of Leicester, and Ambrose Dudley, the Earl of Warwick. Philip's uncles would become two of the most powerful men in Elizabethan England. Leicester in particular was Elizabeth's great favourite and often viewed as prospective husband to the queen. Lady Mary herself served at court as Gentlewoman of the Privy Chamber and nursed Elizabeth through smallpox in 1562, though caught the disease herself and thereafter bore disfiguring facial scars. Sir Henry never let Philip forget his Dudley connection, urging him in an early letter 'Remember, my son, the noble blood you are descended of, by your mother's side; and think that only by virtuous life and good action you shall be an ornament to that illustre family'.[2] Years later, in 1584, when defending Leicester's reputation following a seditious attack in print, Sidney reasserted this connection: 'I am by my father's side of ancient and always well esteemed gentry and well matched gentry, yet I do acknowledge, I say, that my chiefest honour is to be a Dudley, and truly am glad to have cause to set forth the nobility of that blood whereof I am descended' (*MP* 134). As he also discovered, the Dudley connection was a double-edged sword and could often prove disadvantageous. Lady Mary and her father had been engaged in the ill-fated attempt to establish Lady Jane Grey (Mary's sister-in-law) as Edward VI's successor, though the Sidneys escaped the fate of other leading parties involved through their opportune choice of godfather to young Philip.

At several points in his life Sidney was groomed for powerful dynastic marriages, first to Anne, the daughter of Elizabeth's trusted and most powerful councillor, William Cecil, Lord Burghley, and later to Marie of Nassau, daughter of the Dutch Protestant Prince William of Orange. It was also once thought that when the first Earl of Essex, Walter Devereux lay dying in

Ireland in 1576 his last wish was that Sidney marry his daughter Penelope (then aged 11), though evidence for this claim has been called into question.³ (Penelope's role as inspiration for Sidney's sonnet sequence *Astrophil and Stella* is discussed in chapter 4.) Sidney's eventual marriage in 1583 to Frances, daughter of Francis Walsingham, Elizabeth's spymaster and Secretary of State, whilst perhaps not the closest of emotional bonds, maintained Sidney's familial connections with some of the most powerful figures at court.

At the age of 10 Sidney attended Shrewsbury school where he met his lifelong friend Fulke Greville and was educated by Thomas Ashton, a leading humanist pedagogue with excellent Protestant credentials. Sidney entered Christ Church, Oxford, in 1568 where the curriculum further developed his skills in grammar, rhetoric and logic, though he left without taking a degree. In 1572 Leicester sent Sidney as his representative to the French king Charles IX. The embassy provided the springboard for much more extensive travels in Europe, an important final stage in a gentleman's education as Sidney himself wrote to his brother: 'Your purpose is, being a gentleman born, to furnish yourself with the knowledge of such things, as may be serviceable to your country, and fit for your calling'.⁴ Sidney's conduct and family background certainly impressed Charles who made him a baron. In Paris Sidney first met Hubert Languet, the respected Burgundian scholar, diplomat and convert to Protestantism with whom he maintained a regular correspondence for the next nine years. Sidney's time in Paris was also a violent introduction to the volatility of European religious politics and on 24 August, together with the resident ambassador Walsingham, he witnessed the St Bartholomew's Day Massacre in which thousands of Protestants were killed. Sidney was encouraged to return home but was determined to capitalize upon the opportunity to travel widely, drawing on many of Languet's scholarly and political connections and visiting Heidelberg, Frankfurt, Strasburg, Vienna, Hungary, Venice, Padua, Florence, Genoa, Cracow and Prague before returning via Antwerp nearly three years to the day after he left.

The year 1576 saw Sidney begin to embark on the kind of missions for which his experiences in Europe would have prepared him. During the summer he saw first-hand the kind of difficulties his father faced in attempting to administer English rule in Ireland. The English first conquered Ireland in the twelfth century and over time the initial conquerors' descendants (the so-called 'Old English') had to a certain degree integrated with the indigenous Irish and formed an established political and cultural identity of their own. During the sixteenth century a new generation of English colonial personnel – including Sir Walter Raleigh and Edmund Spenser – were tasked to 'complete' the initial conquest and forcibly impose English rule, increasingly, by the 1570s when Sir Henry entered his third term as Lord Deputy, through a policy of enforced plantation of 'New' English settlers and consequent extirpation of the Irish. Where possible Sir Henry used legal and diplomatic, rather than military, means to assert authority, though his progress was limited through lack of financial support. One of Philip's first writings was a defence of his father's policies in Ireland, which seems to have been well received by Elizabeth. Sidney returned from Ireland late in 1576, accompanying the Earl of Essex's body, and soon after received his first real diplomatic mission: to convey the queen's condolences to the Holy Roman Emperor Rudolf II for the death of his father, and to sound him out covertly regarding the formation of a Protestant alliance between Elizabeth and a number of German and Dutch princes. Sidney was widely praised on the continent for his negotiations, though Elizabeth was ultimately wary of promising the level of support that he had suggested and the alliance was never made.

This is an impressive series of accomplishments for the young Sidney that demonstrates his dedication to his family, his country, and his intellectual and political fellow-travellers. But in exploring the nature of Sidney's relationship with the Elizabethan court we should be careful neither to oversimplify our understanding of what a courtier is and does, nor to automatically view everybody employed in the service of the queen or royal household as courtiers. Just as the court as an entity is more usefully thought of as a mobile, intellectual concept defined by the presence of the queen, rather than as a simple physical space, a courtier might best be defined as being one engaged in a particular set of relationships – both with the queen and with others at court in positions of power – rather than as a specific occupation or set of actions. Elizabethan courtship entailed not simply 'being at court' but, as in the more amorous sense of the word, engaging in a complex form of wooing of the monarch or would-be patron. Courtship constituted, as Catherine Bates describes, 'a highly codified system, a series of signs aimed at reassuring the prince or mistress of the suitor's unquestioning and dutiful service. And these signs must be interpreted and decoded correctly in order to manipulate the prince or beloved into making the desired gesture of return'.[5] The courtier was thus defined by their participation in this system of actor and audience, and crucially by the queen's personal recognition and acceptance of this relationship through rewards and preferment. Therefore even works written away from the physical presence of the court, such as Sidney's *Old Arcadia* or Raleigh's poetry written whilst imprisoned in the Tower of London constituted products of court culture.[6] Identity and power at court consisted of a constant process of 'showing' and action, continually reacting to the strategies of others, and of adapting one's verbal and visual techniques of self-presentation in order to capture and control the eyes, ears, conscience and coffers of one's intended audience. The language and pose of the pining lover were used as the basis for one of the fundamental narrative and interpretative games through which power was sought and distributed at court. Power relations are transformed into a Neoplatonic idealized love purged of any physical desire but playing upon the service of a courtly lover. Sidney's writings frequently explore the intersection of political and erotic courtly wooing.

The conscious playing of a role was an important part of the general culture of interpersonal interaction both at the court and in the public stagings of the queen in pageants, tournaments, and on royal progresses. Over the last twenty-five years practitioners of 'new historicism' and its distillates have thoroughly explored the implications of the histrionic or performative nature of identity at Elizabeth's court, of fashioning the self into a work of art. The principal tool in this process was rhetoric, the conscious patterning of one's language to affect, delight and influence one's audience. Early modern schooling and printed rhetoric manuals fostered a reading practice in which appreciation was heavily based on the identification of rhetorical devices or 'figures', diacritical techniques used to embellish one's work through the systematic, deliberate repudiation of everyday speech. Throughout the many (frequently derivative) early modern rhetoric manuals such figures were set out as a series of linguistic devices that could be applied to generate specific effects. For example, in *The Arte of Rhetoric* (1560) Sidney's friend Sir Thomas Wilson describes the figure he calls 'doubtfulness' (*dubitatio*) and its workings:

> Doubtfulness is then used when we make the hearers believe that the weight of our matter causeth us to doubt what were best to speak. As when a king findeth his people unfaithful, he may speak in this wise. 'Before I begin, I doubt what to name ye. Shal I call you subjects? You deserve it not'.[7]

Through the application of rhetorical devices, language was able to exert control over the emotional responses and reasoning of the audience or reader. Rhetoric was conceived of as a tool to manipulate the will of others. Sidney had extensive training in rhetoric at Shrewsbury and Oxford, and apparently translated part of Aristotle's *Rhetoric*, though this is now lost. Although he criticizes such 'paper-books' in the *Defence*, later examples of manuals on rhetoric by John Hoskins and Abraham Fraunce included examples of tropes deployed in Sidney's writings.

There was much similarity between the school manuals of rhetorical devices, the handbooks on poetic composition such as George Puttenham's *Arte of English Poesie* (1589), which also detailed rhetorical tropes and their functions, and the more applied 'grammars' for self-presentation or courtesy books, of which Castiglione's *Book of the Courtier* is the quintessential example. Published in Italian in 1528 (translated into English in 1561), *The Courtier* attempts to define the behaviour and skills fitting for an ideal courtier, all of which should be carried off by adopting the conscious pose of effortless artistry and deliberate effacement of one's industry or labour, known as *sprezzatura*. John Donne admits in his fifth *Satyre* that Castiglione's 'rules' may make good courtiers, but jestingly questions who makes courtiers good, and there is frequent anxiety expressed within and concerning manuals such as *The Courtier* as regards the ultimate utility of eloquence and persuasion at court. While Stephen Greenblatt argues that rhetoric manuals and courtesy books function almost as actors' handbooks, wholly valorizing surface over substance, it is important to remember that Castiglione stresses that the courtier's ultimate goal is not self-centred advancement but that an individual put their skills, abilities and person to the service of their prince and supply good counsel.[8] Such a micro-macrocosmic relationship between individual and monarch, self-improvement and state politics, and private and public interests informs Sidney's conception of both his role at Elizabeth's court and the practical function of his writings. Thus the histrionic relationship between sovereign and courtier was not simply vacuous play-acting. Courtly wooing was also a means of offering counsel, though, as Sidney repeatedly discovers, the queen was certainly not obliged to agree with or accept it.

Throughout early modern Europe royal courts represented the natural point towards which artists, writers and intellectuals gravitated seeking patronage and favour; creative and scholarly endeavour – as now – required nurture and sustained funding. Patronage is also exercised through the aristocracy, and Sidney himself was the dedicatee of over forty works and his family were celebrated patrons of poetry and learning long after his death. It is also frequently suggested that the studied artifice of interpersonal relationships at court and narrative patterning of political interactions were a major factor in the development of literary activity at Elizabeth's court. Although poetry features very little in Castiglione, the qualifications of a thriving courtier – the skill in applied rhetoric, ability to construct a particular stance or voice, and sensitivity to the performative aspect of one's utterance – are also those of the poet. From the 1570s onwards through the occasional verse of courtiers such as the Earl of Oxford, Edward de Vere, and Sir Edward Dyer, poetry, particularly the love lyric, was deployed with increasing frequency within courtly interpersonal interactions. Conventions from the tradition of lovers' complaints modelled on continental vernacular verse by Francis Petrarch and the contemporary French school of poets known as the Pléiade were adapted by Oxford and Dyer to speak of the Elizabethan courtier's situation and the vicissitudes of their mistress's affections and favour. There are many subsequent examples that may be cited where poetry is used as the medium of communication with Elizabeth to advance individual fortunes or negotiate royal disfavour. Dyer's 'Songe in the Oke', for example, presented during the 1575 Woodstock entertainment, appears to have successfully reminded the queen of his presence at court and won him the monopoly for leather tanning. In 'Ocean to Scinthia' Raleigh (writing from prison) cast himself as the despairing lover figure complaining of his beloved's abandonment to reflect on Elizabeth's disfavour towards him following his marriage to Elizabeth Throckmorton in 1592. Puttenham repeatedly stresses the affinity between the art of poetry and skills cultivated at court, including the potentially insincere or deceptive nature of the latter, as he compares allegory to courtly duplicity: 'the courtly figure *allegoria* ... is when we speak one thing and think another, and that our words and our meanings meet not'.[9] Sidney himself interrogates the link between poetry and deception in the *Defence*.

Before proceeding further with discussion of Sidney as a poet it is also important to distinguish between two different early modern models of literary practice: the first is that of the gentlemen amateurs at court, for whom poetry is one of a number of their varied accomplishments, and who wrote for the entertainment of their immediate associates and circulated their work in manuscript, rarely deigning to publish and endure what has been termed the 'stigma of print'.[10] The second is that of a generation of writers (such as Robert Greene, Thomas Nashe, Christopher Marlowe) emerging during the second half of the sixteenth century who sought to 'live by the pen' by writing for the printing press or public theatres in a manner far more akin to our modern literary industry. Sidney was of the former model, publishing virtually nothing during his lifetime. Together with Oxford, Raleigh, Dyer and Greville, he is included among the 'crew of courtly makers – noblemen and gentlemen of her Majesty's own servants', praised by Puttenham, 'who have written excellently well, as it would appear if their doings could be found out and made public with the rest'.[11] Manuscript circulation had the advantage of allowing writers to limit their audience to those they specifically wished to address, and produce their text with an awareness of the physical interface with the ultimate reader. It was a gestural act and means of marking aesthetic, intellectual and ideological affiliations through textual exchange. A modern equivalent might be the difference between sharing an email with a limited number of known correspondents and publishing to the worldwide community on the internet. The social exclusivity of manuscript circulation was often evoked in printed texts by authors wishing to establish claims to gentility or patronage, creating the effect that their work had already been circulated to select numbers. The inclusion of commendatory sonnets in Spenser's *Faerie Queene*, for example, offered written testimony of the text's merit – what publishers now call 'advance praise' – from those already within a supportive network of pre-print circulation.

Some of the most elaborate examples of the Elizabethan 'system' of courtly wooing and narrative interactions were the entertainments staged at the Accession Day tilts, annual tournaments held at Whitehall on 17 November to commemorate the start of Elizabeth's reign, and on the royal progresses, the summer journeys undertaken by the queen and court through the Midlands, south and east of England to visit the nobility and foster political and religious conformity. Sidney was closely involved in the world of courtly gesture and spectacle from a young age and participated in royal tilts and progresses as well as in private entertainments for a coterie audience. He is present at several of Elizabeth's entertainments at Leicester's Kenilworth palace and may have spoken before the queen for the first time there in 1566 at the age of 11. There are also records of Sidney's involvement in the Accession Day festivities from 1577. The tilts were largely ceremonial rather than fiercely competitive martial competitions, an occasion for displaying oneself to the monarch and fellow nobility. They provided the perfect occasion for embracing the fiction casting Elizabeth and her knights as figures from chivalric romance. Participation was very exclusive but tilts were watched by the public from a permanent grandstand at Whitehall. Possibly in an attempt to manoeuvre himself into the position of George Gascoigne's successor as one of the principal craftsmen of court entertainments, Sidney writes two songs for the 1577 tilt (*MW* 2–4). They reveal a familiarity with the representational forms used to celebrate the queen on such occasions, and in casting 17 November as a secular saint's day and fashioning the queen as an object of praise anticipate schemes associated with the cult of the virgin queen developed later in Elizabeth's reign. They also demonstrate how Sidney creates a pastoral persona for himself for use in the ongoing drama of the tilts, a fictional identity going by the patently transparent name of Philisides. The first song has Philisides 'the shepherd good and true' encounter Menalcas (a fellow rustic, whose name commonly appears in classical pastoral) singing praises of his beloved 'Mira'. The relationship of Philisides and Mira is taken up again in Sidney's *Certain Sonnets* collection and *Old Arcadia* eclogues. An eye-witness account of the 1584 tilt records that combatants really were kitted out using devices connected with shepherds and wild men, and Sidney's description of the Iberian jousts in book 2 of the *New Arcadia* (NA 352–7) is frequently compared to contemporary tournament practice.

Sidney's circle were also involved in courtly entertainments. His sister was among the queen's ladies presented with posies of verses by the fairy queen figure at Woodstock in 1575. Despite later rejecting these sorts of occasions in the *Inquisition upon Fame and Honour*, Greville participated in *The Triumph of the Four Foster Children of Desire* (1581) and appears in George Peele's poetic descriptions of the 1590 retirement tilt for Elizabeth's champion Sir Henry Lee, *Polyhymnia*. Dyer and Greville accompany a riderless horse at a solemn ceremony in November 1586 to commemorate Sidney's recent passing. Our principal source of information for the 1595 tilt is a letter from Rowland Whyte to his master, Robert Sidney, serving in the Netherlands at this point; clearly the tilts were considered important home news of which to be kept informed.

Through his increasing participation in entertainments staged during the 1570s and 1580s Sidney learns valuable lessons in how to communicate and function at court through – to use Walter Benjamin's phrase – the 'aestheticization of politics'. Sidney's early entertainments and shows offer a useful model for examining how he conceives of the performance of his works within the public and political sphere, as may be seen from examining two further examples of his shows, one staged for a coterie audience, the other before Elizabeth. In April 1577 Mary Sidney married Henry Herbert, second Earl of Pembroke, and in the summer Philip presented a verse drama at his sister's new home at Wilton, near Salisbury. Sidney's short 'Dialogue between two shepherds' – named Will and Dick – reads initially like one of the many complaints of lovelorn rustics found in the pastoral tradition, such as Virgil's second eclogue. It adopts an outmoded metre known as poulter's measure, rhyming couplets of iambic hexameter followed by iambic heptameter that was popular in early sixteenth-century lyrics. Comedy is soon generated by the disparity between the interlocutors' apparent realization of the formal expectations of the pastoral genre. The dialogue begins with Will endeavouring to cheer his fellow from complaint with suggestions of rural sports. Dick refuses to be persuaded from his melancholy:

> Ah Will, though I grudge not, I count it feeble glee
> With dim sight made dim with daily tears another's sport to see.
> Who ever lambkins saw (yet lambkins love to play)
> To play when that their loved dams are stolen or gone astray?
> If this in them be true, as true in men, think I,
> A lustless song, forsooth, sings he, that hath more lust to cry.
>
> (MW 1)

Dick is determined to play the malcontent lover, but Will needs further explanation as to the cause of Dick's 'darkness': 'What, is thy bagpipe broke, or are thy lambs miswent,/ Thy wallet or thy tar-box lost, or thy new raiment rent?' These are all very pragmatic responses, the sort of issues a real-life shepherd might have. However, pastoral poetry has very little to do with the quotidian affairs of everyday shepherds. As Puttenham asserted, the self-evident artifice of pastoral – the presentation of philosophical, literary and political discussion through shepherds' mouths – made it the most appropriate vehicle for publicly 'speaking the other':

> the poet devised the eclogue...not of purpose to counterfeit or represent the rustical manner of loves and communications, but under the veil of homely persons, and in rude speechs to insinuate and glance at greater matters, and such as perchance had not been safe to have been disclosed in any other sort.[12]

Sidney himself writes in the *Defence* that a pastoralist 'under the pretty tales of wolves and sheep, can include the whole considerations of wrong-doing and patience' (MW 229). The intrinsically unmimetic nature of pastoral provided a self-conscious means of saying other things. Pastoral was thus an entirely apposite form in which to present figurative reflections upon the dilatory otium of Elizabethan court life. In his poem 'Disprayse of Court Life' Sidney adopts a shepherd's persona to contrast court life negatively with pastoral innocence, his only pleasure at court being his companions Dyer and Greville. 'Shepherd' became something of a synonym for poet at Elizabeth's court and the pastoral conceit was often used to represent the community of writers engaged in 'piping' for the queen, as in Spenser's *Colin Clouts Come Home Againe* or his elegy for Sidney, *Astrophel* (both 1595).

The comedy of Sidney's dialogue lies in the fact that Dick's part is clearly written with this self-consciousness in mind; but Will seems far less attuned to the conventions of the genre, to what he ought to be doing. As Dick sets out his lamentable state ('a mistress I do serve/ Whose wages makes me beg the more, who feeds me till I starve/ Whose livery is such as most I freeze, apparelled most'), Will can only scratch his head, professing 'These are riddles, sure'. Dick is forced at each stage to decode the metaphor concerning his amorous service to his unnamed beloved, whilst Will remains doggedly incapable of seeing things beyond a purely economic relationship. Following Dick's exposition of his seemingly tyrannical mistress, Will's reaction remains that of a worried shepherd. The dialogue concludes with Will's eventual realization of the possible presence of a third party to their exchange as he says 'let us go hence, lest we great folks annoy'. Exit Dick and Will; cue polite applause from 'great folks' such as Mary and her husband. Sidney plays here with the boundaries between persona or acted part and the context of performance. Even in this simple, early dialogue he explores the relationship between figurative and literal interpretation, between opacity and transparency of metaphor. Sidney also highlights the interpretative potential of pastoral here and the pleasure to be derived from interpreting pastoral. After all, nobody wants to be seen reading pastoral with the limited vision of Will. Mary complemented Philip's piece with her own 'Dialogue between two shepheards, Thenot and Piers, in praise of Astrea', written for a planned, though aborted royal visit to Wilton in 1599 and later published in Francis Davison's collection *A Poetical Rapsody* (1602).

In May 1578 the queen stayed at Wanstead, Essex, one of Leicester's recent acquisitions. Records of progresses and entertainments repeatedly portray the implausibly mythical nature of the landscape through which Elizabeth annually journeyed, happening upon satyrs, nymphs, and wild-men while hunting on her nobles' estates, hearing orations from shepherds or classical gods gathered seemingly by chance. Like a character from the very texts used to represent and glorify her, Elizabeth encountered and engaged with a host of mythical and allegorical characters in a fusion of life and art. One such encounter initiates Sidney's masque *The Lady of May*:

> Her most excellent Majesty walking in Wanstead Garden, as she passed down into the grove, there came suddenly among the train one apparelled like an honest man's wife of the country...crying out for justice, and desiring all the lords and gentlemen to speak a good word for her. (*MW* 5)

The figure asks the queen's aid in a contention between two suitors for the hand of her daughter, the chosen local Lady of May or may queen. The first suitor is Therion (whose name means 'wild creature'), a forester who, though the livelier of the two, is also prone to railing against and striking the lady; the other, Espilus (literally, 'felt-presser', one working with wool or cloth), is richer, though a little more dull. In Sidney's words he is 'of a mild disposition', never doing great service or great ill, but spending most of the time feeding his sheep or recording the lady's name in 'doleful verses'. The disputants are introduced by a local schoolmaster, Master Rombus, whose pedantic Latinate annotations of the evolving debate parodies the stilted orations presented to Elizabeth by university men. Gabriel Harvey would present such an oration at Audley End the same summer, and Shakespeare may allude to Rombus through the character Holofernes in *Love's Labours Lost*, a play all about courtly diversions and demotic entertainments. Like figures in a staged combat, the verbal pugilists have their 'seconds' or supporters, the forester Rixus and shepherd Dorcas.

All parties in the entertainment aggressively implore the queen to pass judgement in their debate, combining an appeal to the queen's faculties of discernment with candid admission of the great awe and power engendered by her presence. The opening supplication, for example, refers to how Elizabeth's face 'doth oft the bravest sort enchant' and how 'Your face hurts oft, but still it doth delight' (*MW* 5–6). There is awareness of the potential doubleness of royal power, the capacity to reward or punish. References to the royal 'sight' and presence again celebrate the specific occasion of performance that a printed version of the text can only recreate secondhand, and continue to modulate between the presented narrative and the temporal performative context. Through the pastoral commonplace of the singing contest, Therion, Espilus and their supporters argue the respective merits of an active, more swashbuckling woodman's life versus the more passive, secure, contemplative shepherd's life. Therion actually appears to embody both and is clearly the party Sidney favours and wants Elizabeth to choose. After a summing-up by Rombus and the Lady, onus for judgement is placed upon Elizabeth, who chooses Espilus, though 'what words, what reasons she used for it', we are told (conveniently), 'this paper, which carrieth so base names, is not worthy to contain' (*MW* 12). Many topical interpretations of this judgement are possible. Some critics see Espilus as a safe, domesticated version of Leicester. Others interpret Therion's praise of the active life as a call for greater involvement in the politics of the Netherlands, where the Dutch were increasingly beleaguered by the occupying Spanish and looked for support to the militant Protestant faction at Elizabeth's court centred on Leicester. In such a reading Sidney's entertainment failed because Elizabeth chose 'incorrectly'. Direct identification of either disputant is problematic, however, not least because the narrative clearly points to Leicester as a third-party figure situated at the text's boundaries, 'a certain gentleman' located nearby. In a concluding passage in one manuscript of the masque, Rombus later identifies him as 'Master Robert of Wanstead' who is almost papist in his praise of Elizabeth: 'I have found *unum par*, a pair, *papisticorum bedorum*, of Papistian beads, *cum quos*, with the which *omnium dierum*, every day, next after his *pater noster* he *semper* saith "and Elizabeth", as many lines as there be beads on this string' (*MW* 13). Sidney allows Elizabeth to select her own ending in *The Lady of May* and as in any disputation, where he was trained to contend both sides of an argument, he incorporates a conclusion that supports either decision made. It is also vital to remember that the text records an event that has already occurred, and that Sidney can have the last word in the written version to make the best of Elizabeth's ultimate judgement, concluding the masque with a statement of Leicester's fealty. The text allows Sidney and his uncle's faction to present difficult issues and questions to the queen, to model alternatives and sound her out, to voice oppositional policies allowing (perhaps necessitating) the queen to make a decision, and playfully attempt to garner a straight answer. The *Old Arcadia* and *Four Foster Children of Desire* see Sidney's writings playing a similar role in anatomizing Elizabeth's proposed marriage to Francis, Duc d'Anjou.

Sidney's own politics place him nearer to Therion's camp than that of 'idle' Espilus; only the month before, Johann Casimir, Count Palatine, requested that Sidney lead an army to the Netherlands. Within the binary structure of *The Lady of May* Sidney sets the life of political action embodied by Therion in opposition to one of pastoral complaint, suggesting that pastoral contemplation acts as a conscious displacement for active employment. Dorcus's arguments stress how appropriate their life is as a means of expressing courtiers' complaints:

> How many courtiers, think you, I have heard under our field in bushes make their woeful complaints, some of the greatness of their mistress' estate, which dazzled their eyes and yet burned their hearts; some of the extremity of her beauty mixed with extreme cruelty; some of her too much wit, which made all their loving labours folly ... So that with long lost labour, finding their thoughts bare no other wool but despair, of young courtiers they grew shepherds. (*MW* 11)

But whilst he may have preferred the 'gallant sort of activity' embodied by Therion, Sidney's entertainment nevertheless argues that the pastoral form offers a valid rhetorical alternative to physical displays of active virtue. *The Lady of May* is one of the first works of pastoral entertainment employed in celebration of Elizabeth and a key text in establishing a central mythographic persona for the queen – the pastoral mistress – and an expressive medium through which subjects could employ bucolic otium as a figure for court life and their relationship to the queen. Indeed, in the *Old Arcadia* Sidney contrives that the origins of pastoral itself lie in such royal sports.

Sidney's entertainments were well received in his own day. Edmund Molyneux's biography of Sidney, included in Holinshed's 1587 *Chronicles,* observes that 'at jousts, triumphs, and other such royal pastimes (for at all such disports he commonly made one) he would bring in such a lively gallant show, so agreeable to every point, which is required for the expressing of a perfect device (so rich was he in those inventions)' (*MW* 314). Writing in 1584 the Italian Protestant Scipio Gentili claimed that Sidney's public entertainments were his greatest achievements. Sidney is clearly familiar with the vocabulary of images, mythological schemes, and panegyric strategies found in Elizabethan entertainments. His works embrace the range of different forms that these take: tilt narratives, recitations, orations, and disputations. By no means simply apprentice-pieces, the shows and entertainments Sidney witnessed and latterly participated in are important creative influences upon the more well-known texts, not least because – when Sidney offers his own contributions – they are conceived and composed in concert with early versions of works such as the *Old Arcadia.* There is a tendency in Sidney criticism to assert a rigid distinction between the public and private aspects of Sidney's life and assign his literary interests almost wholly to the latter. For some, his poetry is associated with freedom and represents the antithesis of court, drawing a line between the coterie poet, writing largely at Wilton, and the courtier poet. Certainly Sidney felt a greater sense of leisure and liberty at Wilton. We should not baulk, however, at examining public presentations, such as the tilt songs and royal entertainments, in relation to the more private, domestic pieces penned (initially) for reception within the Wilton coterie; pieces such as the 1577 pastoral dialogue and the *Old Arcadia*. It is productive therefore to explore similarities and continuities in form and, crucially, rhetorical stance across the Sidney corpus. The paradigm of coterie and court performance and presentation – of playing out a text to a realized or implied audience – informs Sidney's work throughout his short career, and offers great insight into how he conceives of the workings of allegory and the relationship between temporal context and figural representation. The construction of fictional alter egos and personae for himself and his immediate audience, the modelling of performative scenarios whereby figures or characters are seen playing out a narrative to a courtly audience, and the continual invitations for the audience/reader to move between literal and allegorical interpretations of the text, are all features of the Wilton and Wanstead shows that also form a key part of the composition and reception of Sidney's 'read' texts.

2

Arcadian Toys

According to Edmund Molyneux, Sidney began work on the *Old Arcadia* upon returning from Europe in 1577 'before his further employment by her Majesty, at his vacant and spare times of leisure (for he could endure at no time to be idle and void of action)' (*MW* 311), though there are suggestions that he was interested in literary pursuits somewhat earlier. During the 1577 embassy German poet Paulus Melissus proclaimed in verse 'O, Sidney, renowned for your study of the Muses', and sometime travelling companion Lodowick Bryskett mentions that Sidney was 'with the Muses sporting' during their earlier continental tour.[1] By 1579 Daniel Rogers praises Sidney's accomplishments as a fellow poet and alludes to literary collaborations with Dyer and Greville. The following year, when he started the *Defence*, Sidney adopted the modest pose (wonderfully illustrative of *sprezzatura*) of having 'slipped into the title of a poet', and being 'provoked to say something unto you in the defence of that my unelected vocation' (*MW* 212). It should be stressed that Sidney nowhere signals an intention to become a published poet or live by the pen, but there is increasing evidence from the late 1570s onwards of his sustained experimentation with English versification and exploration of poetry's utility that went beyond the level of simple compliance with what was expected of a cultured courtier.

As Molyneux suggests, the *Old Arcadia* was composed during enforced leisure, a dilatory period in which Elizabeth repeatedly obstructed Sidney's plans for greater English support for continental Protestants and grew increasingly unwilling to assign Sidney to duties overseas due to her distrust of his evident popularity with foreign rulers. Sidney spent much of this leisure at his sister's house at Wilton. The political and intellectual community that developed at Wilton was hugely important in providing a physical and mental space away from court in which much of Sidney's writing takes shape. The immediate contexts of the *Old Arcadia*'s production and reception at Wilton are described in the dedication to the Mary Sidney prefacing of the 1590 edition:

> Here now have you (most dear, and most worthy to be most dear lady) this idle work of mine, which I fear (like the spider's web) will be thought fitter to be swept away than worn to any other purpose. For my part, in very truth (as the cruel fathers among the Greeks were wont to do to the babes they would not foster) I could well find in my heart to cast out in some desert of forgetfulness this child which I am loathe to father. But you desired me to do it, and your desire to my heart is an absolute commandment. Now it is done only for you, only to you; if you keep it to yourself, or to such friends who will weigh errors in the balance of goodwill, I hope, for the father's sake, it will be pardoned, perchance made much of, though in itself it have deformities. For indeed, for severer eyes it is not, being but a trifle, and that triflingly handled. Your dear self can best witness the manner, being done in loose sheets of paper, most of it in your presence, the rest by sheets sent unto you as fast as they were done. (*OA* 3)

Two things stand out here. Firstly, the generative metaphors used to describe the work's composition and emergence make playful reference to Mary's pregnancy during the final stages of the writing process in 1580. More laboured, however, are the repeated references to the text as a work of idleness, a 'trifle, and that triflingly handled'. In a letter to his brother, Sidney refers to the *Old Arcadia* as his 'toyfull book'. But we should be wary of taking these apparently throwaway comments at face value. For a start the dedication quoted above does not appear in any extant *Old Arcadia* manuscript and may have been included by Greville in an attempt to fashion a distinction between such worldly 'toys' and Sidney's more religious works, upon which Greville wished to base his friend's posthumous reputation. Idleness is a major concern both for characters within Arcadia and for Sidney himself in writing the *Old Arcadia*. It is explored throughout the text as Sidney's rustication, and attendant anxieties regarding the utility of his own enforced leisure, are juxtaposed with the pastoral retreat of Duke Basilius and the princes Musidorus and Pyrocles and their apparently trivial pastimes in Arcadia. As with Sidney's use of pastoral at Wilton and Wanstead, the veil of 'homely persons' (to use Puttenham's phrase) could be employed to 'glance at greater matters'.

The *Old Arcadia* is best described as a pastoral romance, though it draws together materials from many different sources to form an innovative synthesis of genres and modes: pastoral and heroic, narrative and dramatic, poetry and prose. In the *Defence* Sidney remains equivocal towards works of mixed mode, offering muted acknowledgement that 'some poesies have coupled together two or three kinds' and that 'if severed they be good, the conjunction cannot be hurtful', though criticizing tragi-comic plays for violating generic decorum (*MW* 228–9). Nevertheless, the clash of different generic expectations is fundamental to the *Old Arcadia*'s construction and narrative method. Kings and clowns do indeed mingle in Arcadia. For his work's title and his idealized landscape populated by singing shepherds Sidney looked to Jacopo Sannazaro's immensely popular *Arcadia* (1504), a series of twelve poetic eclogues linked by twelve prose passages. Of greater influence upon the subject matter and plot was Jorge de Montemayor's *Diana* (1559), a Spanish prose romance with occasional poems that combined the setting and tone of classical pastoral with the action of medieval chivalric romance. The hybrid generic landscape of pastoral romance was the setting for many Elizabethan entertainments, such as Gascoigne's tale of Hemetes the hermit presented at Woodstock in 1575, which – like the *Old Arcadia* – drew upon Greek romances such as Heliodorus's *Æthiopica* (English translation 1569). Heliodorus's story of betrothed lovers Theagenes and Chariclea concluded with a trial of their sexual mores that anticipates book 5 of the *Old Arcadia*. Sidney's main plot concerning Pyrocles's disguise and amorous adventures was based on an episode from the vast prose romance *Amadis de Gaule* (originally Spanish; French translation 1540–48) in which Prince Agesilan falls in love with Diane via a portrait and, together with his cousin, adopts a female disguise to woo his beloved. Sidney's debt to English sources should not be overlooked. The intrusive narrator and five-part structure centred on the consummation of lovers recall Chaucer's *Troilus and Criseyde* and Sidney's text continues the interrogation of the complexities and contradictions of chivalry pursued in Malory's *Morte Darthur*. There are further echoes of Malory in the *New Arcadia* in character-names such as the Knight of the Tomb and the Black Knight, which supports (otherwise unsubstantiated) claims by Ben Jonson's friend William Drummond that Sidney intended to transform 'all his Arcadia to the stories of King Arthur'.

The complex 'interlace' plot structure of the *Arcadias* (*Old* and *New*) and active narratorial management of different strands of action were heavily influenced by Italian romance-epic, particularly Ludovico Ariosto's *Orlando Furioso* (1532). Sixteenth-century scholarly controversy developed around the relative merit and utility of the romance form. Humanists such as Roger Ascham condemned such works as vacuous products of idleness ('bookes of fayned cheualrie, wherin a man by redinge, shuld be led to none other ende, but onely to manslaughter and baudrye') and romance was frequently derided as a trivial form suitable only for female amusement.[2] In response, attempts were made to rehabilitate or moralize romance and later editions of Ariosto included elaborate allegorical glosses identifying virtuous examples and lessons. Allegory played an important part in redefining the moral utility of romance, and writers and translators of romance-epic such as Torquato Tasso and Sir John Harington (the latter familiar with Sidney's work) went to great lengths to negotiate anxieties concerning the fanciful and fantastic in the form. The *Old Arcadia*, and Sidney's prefatory comments on idleness, must therefore be viewed within the context of this ongoing theorization on how romance might provide moral instruction.

Ostensibly the *Old Arcadia*'s story is quite simple. The prophecy heard by Arcadia's ruler Basilius at the start functions rather like the argument of the work, mapping out in enigmatically ambivalent terms what we will see take place:

> Thy elder care shall from thy careful face
> By princely mean be stolen and yet not lost;
> Thy younger shall with nature's bliss embrace
> An uncouth love, which nature hateth most.
> Thou with thy wife adult'ry shalt commit,
> And in thy throne a foreign state shall sit.
> All this on thee this fatal year shall hit.

(*OA* 5)

The main plot centres on princes Musidorus and Pyrocles as they attempt to woo Basilius's daughters Pamela and Philoclea, the confusions arising from their respective disguises as shepherd Dorus and Amazon Cleophila, their heroic conduct when faced with marauding beasts and rebels, and their final trial following the apparent poisoning of Basilius. Between each book eclogues record the singing contests of the princes and Arcadian shepherds, the majority of whom have little part in the prose narrative. Incorporating some of Sidney's earliest poetry, the eclogues provide a choric reflection on the main themes of each book: the first focus on unrequited love; the second debate reason versus passion; the third ideals of married love; the fourth death and loss. It is in the eclogues that much of Sidney's experimentation with English versification takes place, though the *Old Arcadia* as whole represents a virtuoso display of different forms, including: the blazon (*OA* 28, 207); Anacreontics (*OA* 143); echo songs (*OA* 140–42); epithalamia (*OA* 201); dream vision (*OA* 291); trisyllabic rhyme or *sdrucciola* (*OA* 121–4); and a sonnet where every line rhymes on '-ight' (*OA* 159). Sidney introduces a number of new poetic forms into English, as in his much-discussed double sestina 'Ye goat-herd gods' (*OA* 285–7), in which each of the twelve stanzas utilize the same terminal words for each line, though in different combinations. Sidney also included experiments with vernacular quantitative verse, attempting to fit classical rules for scansion based on the length of syllables to English poetry (*OA* 71–8). Spenser and Harvey claimed to have corresponded with Sidney and Dyer on English hexameters and formulated 'Lawes and rules' for native quantitative verse as part of a coterie called the Areopagus (named after the Athenian parliament), though the level of intimacy between Sidney and Spenser is unclear. Proponents of quantitative and qualitative verse (structured by rhyme) contested the merits of each form throughout the later sixteenth century. Sidney discusses the debate in the *Defence*, though fails to indicate a preference for either form (*MW* 249).

Symmetry and parallelism are important structural devices in the *Old Arcadia*. Sidney's narrator skilfully manages the distinct narrative strands dealing with each of the princes' convoluted amorous adventures, at times comparing their fortunes or having them meet to update the other on their progress, at others demonstrating the different problems encountered by each, resulting from their disguised class or gender, whilst attempting to woo their respective beloved. With similar care Sidney crafts each book so as to signal both the growing complexity of the double love-plot and the increasing severity of the intrusions upon Basilius's retreat. In book 1 the biggest challenge the princes face is the lion and she-bear, which are easily defeated. In book 2 the Phagonian rebels pose a much greater threat, though again through tongue and sword the princes save the day. The princes (particularly Pyrocles) are equally successful in their amorous escapades by the close of book 3. By the end of book 4, however, events have become graver, with Basilius apparently murdered and the princes unable to fight or talk their way out of imprisonment. Sidney divides the *Old Arcadia* into five 'books or acts', and the latter term explains his overall organization of the work. Several critics have argued that Sidney improves on the often fragmentary, episodic nature of heroic poetry by adopting a coherent, unified five-act structure found in Terentian comedy. The comedies of Roman playwright Terence (as expounded upon by fourth-century grammarian Donatus) were divided into *protasis* (introduction of characters, exposition of plot and beginning of intrigue), *epitasis* (complication of plot), and *catastrophe* (resolution through which tragedy is ultimately averted). The *Old Arcadia* certainly fits such a pattern, with books 1 and 2 as *protasis*, 3 and 4 as *epitasis*, and book 5 as the *catastrophe*. Within individual books of the *Old Arcadia* Sidney continues to demonstrate his mastery of intricate plot construction; witness Pyrocles's manipulation of Basilius and Gynecia's 'adulterous' rendezvous or Musidorus's multiple trickery on Dametas and family, which are executed with the polished precision of Chaucerian fabliaux.

Sidney's prose style has an equally playful, copious quality that frequently heightens the sense of melodrama in the narrative, but this does not necessarily make things easy for a modern reader. The book's opening lines immediately present a challenge: a long sentence revealing the influence of Latin syntax that breaks down into carefully balanced clauses and subclauses, some of which are subordinated to one another and linked by subordinating conjunctions (a concept known as *hypotaxis*) and some of which are linked by coordinating conjunctions such as 'and' or 'but' (*parataxis*):

> Arcadia among all the provinces of Greece was ever had in singular reputation, partly for the sweetness of the air and other natural benefits, but principally for the moderate and well tempered minds of the people who (finding how true a contentation is gotten by following the course of nature, and how the shining title of glory, so much affected by other nations, doth indeed help little to the happiness of life) were the only people which, as by their justice and providence gave neither cause nor hope to their neighbours to annoy them, so were they not stirred with false praise to trouble others' quiet, thinking it a small reward for the wasting of their own lives in ravening that their posterity should long after say they had done so. (*OA* 4)

The effect is one of a continued intensification of description and qualification, and a self-conscious display of syntactic control. Sidney's prose style here is often contrasted with that known as Euphuism, the mannerist use of alliteration and similes from natural history initiated by John Lyly's *Euphues* (1578), which Sidney rejects in the *Defence* and *Astrophil*. But Sidney is just as fond of rhetorical excesses in the *Old Arcadia* and he repeatedly indulges in a host of rhetorical devices to adorn his prose: antithesis, descriptive catalogues, personifications, epithets, repetitions. Sidney, like Lyly, particularly favoured the extended simile as a tool of ornamentation, despite observing in the *Defence* that they serve more to illustrate than persuade. See, for example, his comparison of Philoclea's swelling sense of joy whilst hearing of Pyrocles's adventures to that of Pygmalion as he slowly crafts Galatea, or the way that Musidorus drops everything to save Pamela as fast as a schoolboy discards his toy at the presence of a feared schoolmaster (*OA* 106, 267). At times Sidney's language anticipates the extravagant conceits of metaphysical verse; for example when Musidorus imagines Pamela's teeth beneath her lips: 'through them the eye of his fancy delivered to his memory the lying (as in ambush) under her lips of those armed ranks, all armed in most pure white, and keeping the most precise order of military discipline' (*OA* 177). Sidney's prose, it is sometimes remarked, is poetry in all but form.

One could easily cite numerous illustrations of different rhetorical devices deployed in Sidney's text; Fraunce's *Arcadian Rhetorike* (1588) gives over eighty examples of tropes and figures used in the *Old Arcadia*. But it is perhaps more important to consider how language and rhetoric are not simply a medium and means of ornament in the text but are fundamental to what the *Old Arcadia* is 'about'. Characters are forever presenting speeches, debates and singing contests. Rhetorical occasions are Sidney's essential building block in the *Old Arcadia*. The opening scene shows Philanax's vain attempt to counsel Basilius against his rural retirement, using a model of formal rhetoric couched in terms of what Philanax *would* have said to his lord had advice been sought (a technique called *occupatio*). Almost immediately Sidney demonstrates the limitations of rhetoric: that, however learned one's advice may be, there is always the danger a ruler will pursue their own folly regardless, particularly where that ruler accepts counsel merely 'for fashion's sake'. This initial failure of rhetoric leads on to the next key debate: Musidorus and Pyrocles's argument about the relative merits of an active life of 'worthy enterprises' versus the more contemplative – potentially idle – life of pursuing love. If we read the duke's interpretation of the oracle as his argument advocating retirement the opening interaction between Basilius and Philanax could be construed as a dialogue. Both sides of the princes' debate are far more developed. Musidorus's concern is the transformative power of love, and he argues that 'this effeminate love of a woman doth so womanize a man' and distracts Pyrocles from his active 'main career'. Pyrocles – no doubt to Sidney's immediate audience's approval – retorts with a defence of female virtue, and proceeds to use the Neoplatonic argument that temporal love of an individual is the first stage of an ascent to apprehending heavenly love (*OA* 20). Neoplatonism was widely used in Renaissance love poetry, including Donne's 'The Ecstasy' and Spenser's *Fowre Hymnes*. Of course, Pyrocles's later, very worldly preoccupations put into doubt his commitment to such lofty sentiments, as we see, for example, when Philoclea flees the bear:

> her nymphlike apparel being carried up with the wind, that much of those beauties she would at another time have willingly hidden were presented to the eye of the twice-wounded Cleophila; which made Cleophila not follow her over hastily lest she should too soon deprive herself of that pleasure. (*OA* 43)

Just as at Wanstead, it is limiting to view the princes' debate in crude terms of winners and losers. Sidney is more interested in considering *both* sides of the argument, not least because it provides an analogy with the wider question as to whether love is a fit subject for his own writing.

There are many other examples of disputations and arguments in the *Old Arcadia*: Pyrocles's oration to the rebels; the wooing scenes in book 3; Pyrocles and Philoclea's debate on suicide. The final book returns rhetoric to its judicial origins as Philanax indicts Gynecia, Pyrocles and Musidorus for Basilius's death and his daughters' rape. Each prince attempts to counter Philanax's accusations, and Musidorus refers back to both princes' valiant service to Arcadia that surely demonstrates their worthiness as legitimate suitors. Malory's Lancelot uses a similar argument to defend his adultery with Guinevere, though extended formal debate in chivalric romance is otherwise rare. As in the two debates that establish the principal action of the *Old Arcadia*, the issue of 'winning' the trial is secondary to the exploration of the issues, or at least it is made so by the *deus ex machina* conclusion that sees Basilius wake and the princes exonerated. By placing rhetoric at the heart of his romance Sidney begins to rehabilitate the form, to question the commonplaces of the genre even as they are deployed, especially those relating to love and personal desire and their place in state affairs. In Arcadia Sidney creates an imaginative, interrogative space in which to model and experiment with different ideas relating to poetry and politics, and in particular to explore the relation between the two.

One of the principal agents in this interrogative process is Sidney's narrator. The narrator – or Sidney's narratorial voice – provides continual reminders of the imagined scenario of his playing out the story to his sister and her ladies.[3] The quasi-dramatic mode of presentation anticipates the chatty narrators of early novelists Lawrence Sterne and Henry Fielding, but Sidney's narration plays upon his relationship with a known audience, breaking off on occasions to directly address 'You ladies' of the Wilton coterie. The narrator compounds the playful nature of the *Old Arcadia*, offering parenthetic asides and additional information, making sententious observations on his story, and emphasizing the management of his characters, as when he switches attention between his heroes' respective adventures in book 3: 'But Cleophila (whom I left in the cave hardly bested, having both great wits and stirring passions to deal with) makes me lend her my pen awhile to see with what dexterity she could put by her dangers' (*OA* 177). Sidney is not above titillating his audience or making them blush as they momentarily share a male character's amorous viewpoint, for instance when Pyrocles first espies Philoclea: 'her body covered with a light taffeta garment, so cut as the wrought smock came through it in many places (enough to have made a very restrained imagination have thought what was under it)' (*OA* 34). The text is full of wry descriptions and asides clearly designed to provoke an amused response from Sidney's initial audience. At times the narrator demonstrates great familiarity with characters' thoughts and motives and a sympathy with their predicament, seen most obviously when he signals that he will refer to Pyrocles as Cleophila while 'she' adopts the Amazonian disguise (*OA* 25). But the distance between the narrator and his story continually shifts and Sidney frequently provides both comedy and commentary in the *Old Arcadia* through his ironic detachment from his characters. At one point Sidney adopts the authorial role of a *compilator* – one who assembles and transmits the words of others – in contriving to use the 'ancient records of Arcadia' to tell of the bear's fate (*OA* 46).

Sidney seldom passes judgement on his characters' actions and motives, preferring instead to present models of both virtue and folly and use the ambivalence this creates as an interrogative tool, framing questions that must be applied and answered outside of the text. The opening description of Basilius ('a prince of *sufficient* skill to govern so quiet a country where the good minds of the former princes had set down good laws' (emphasis mine)) subtly suggests a certain limitation of his powers, and represents the start of more extensive questioning and challenging of the duke's fitness to rule. One finds similar distance evoked in the scene where Musidorus is about to rape Pamela but '(to the just punishment of his broken promise, and most infortunate bar of his long-pursued and almost-achieved desires) there came by a dozen clownish villains' (*OA* 177). The ambiguous description of the interruption as both 'just' and 'infortunate' situates the narrator uneasily between condemnation and complicity. The first three books of the *Old Arcadia* encourage the reader's sympathy with the princes' increasingly questionable erotic adventures before books 4 and 5, through the involvement of Euarchus, force a reassessment and condemnation of their actions. Again we are situated into positions of both complicity and judgement. As Sidney's most recent biographer writes, the text was written 'to provoke questions, not necessarily to answer them. It provides a record not of Philip's consistent political philosophy, but of his ongoing intellectual enquiry'.[4] It is this continuing sense of enquiry that led Sidney to revise the *Old Arcadia*.

It is not only through disputations within the *Old Arcadia* that Sidney provokes questions. The interrogative impulse is also maintained by the consciously polysemic nature of the work and the inclusion of episodes – from Basilius's failed reading of the prophecy onwards – centred on characters and objects requiring interpretation, signification and unveiling. This takes many forms. One of the most obvious is the transparent allusion Sidney makes to himself. In addition to his omniscient, first-person narrator figure, Sidney includes his own fictional alter ego Philisides as a character in the text, who has already been mentioned in relation to the tilt narratives and the persona Sidney adopted for entertainments at around the same time he wrote the *Old Arcadia*. Sidney evidently imitated Sannazaro, who includes his surrogate Sincero in his *Arcadia* and similarly plays upon his own name. Sidney continues to provide onomastic reminders of himself through the names of Philanax, Philoclea and Antiphilus. Philisides's account of his life in the fourth eclogues presents a veiled autobiography of Sidney himself. Many critics have continued the interpretative game and attempted to decipher the identity of Philisides's beloved Mira who constitutes the central focus of the character's poetry. Philisides's courtship of Mira has already taken place by the time of events presented in the *Old Arcadia*. It can be traced in a number of poems that were produced alongside the romance and completed by 1580: the 1577 tilt song; Sonnets 8–11 in *Certain Sonnets*; and Song 5 of *Astrophil*. By Philisides's final eclogue Mira is clearly beyond his grasp and he is driven to despair by her devotion to a chaste life that precludes his suit, and the sequence sees Sidney adapt the paradigmatic narrative arc of desire, rejection and loss found in the earlier court poetry of Dyer, Oxford and Gascoigne, to which he returns in *Astrophil*. The Philisides–Mira courtship is both allusive and elusive. Mira has been identified as Penelope Devereux, though she was not at court at this point, and as another unidentified object of Sidney's affections, possibly one of Elizabeth's attendants (Philisides describes her as Diana's 'waiting nymph' (*OA* 293)). She has also been interpreted as Sidney's sister Mary and as the queen herself, though no single identification satisfactorily addresses the many aspects of Mira portrayed or the range of responses she invites; calls for revenge against her in Song 5, for example, would be unwise if she were Elizabeth. Mira can be read most productively as an abstract object of 'wonder' (her name deriving from the Latin for 'wonder') and desired source of favour, the stimulus for a way of talking about a particular relationship, be it amorous or political. Greville also uses the Mira figure in over a dozen poems to articulate his own reworking of Petrarchan conventions.

Like the narrator, Philisides's presence serves as a reminder of the moment of authorship and textual presentation, of the world outside of the text. This is clearly seen in the third eclogues, where he recites the beast fable learned from 'old Languet' (*OA* 221–5), the most direct identification with a real person made in the *Old Arcadia*, though one still couched in pastoral terms. The poem was professedly learned on the banks of the Ister (the Danube) and alludes to Sidney and Languet's time together in Vienna during 1573–4. The poem is an allegory on how the golden age in which only animals lived on earth is shattered when they decide they need a king, who, once they have fashioned him in the form of man and endowed him with their best attributes, reduces them all to servitude. With characteristic eclecticism Sidney draws upon Aesop and Ovid together with the story of the Israelites' desire for a king from 1 Samuel 8. Beast fable, like pastoral, self-consciously invites interpretation as it is a patently unmimetic form (since animals do not act like this in real life) and, as amongst Philisides's initial audience, the poem has attracted 'diverse judgements' on exactly what is meant. Sidney presents not only a mythologized aetiology of monarchy, but an admonition against tyranny – where the public good of a kingdom suffers through a ruler's selfish pursuit of private desires, a state not dissimilar to that imposed by Basilius. The closing allusions to how common beasts suffered once the nobler beasts were killed by man is frequently interpreted as referring to how the aristocracy should function as a safeguard for the liberty of the commonwealth against monarchical tyranny. The ascription of this poem to Languet signals its affinity to contemporary Protestant resistance literature, such as the 1579 *Vindiciae contra tyrannos* ('Defence Against Tyrants'), produced by Languet and his Huguenot associates concerning limited monarchy and a sovereign's duty to their subjects. Initially this literature defended resistance to Spanish occupation of the Netherlands but also represented dangerous textual weapons if applied in England or France to existing controversy on relationships between aristocratic and monarchical authority. Again, under 'pretty tales of wolves and sheep', Sidney registers his engagement with weighty matters relating to international politics which are anything but trifling.

Like the staged entertainments, Sidney's Arcadian world repeatedly invites us to shift between literal and figurative interpretation. Characters are seen veiling themselves and in turn being 'decoded' by other characters: while Pyrocles's disguise is opaque to some, Gynecia soon sees through his Amazon outward appearance (*OA* 43), and great mirth is made of his multiple 'readings' by others. Similarly, Musidorus decodes himself in revealing his identity to Pamela, shifting from description of his actions in the third person to a first-person admission that the 'dolorous tale' he recites is actually his own (*OA* 93). Shepherds throughout Arcadia sing of how their outwardly joyful countenance hides their inward hurt. In addition to the 'hidden forms' employed in the eclogues to utter 'such matter as otherwise were not fit for their delivery' (*OA* 50), there are many episodes inviting direct interpretation from the reader: emblematic images, such as Pamela's jewel depicting a chained lamb (*OA* 34) or Dicus's rustic heraldry showing Cupid as a hangman (*OA* 57); dream visions, such as of Gynecia and Philisides (*OA* 103, 291–6); and onomastic clues suggestive of how to read a character or place. The Phagonian rebels, for example, take their name from Greek *phagon* or 'glutton' and it is their drunken revels that initiate the revolt.

Similar etymological play is found with the central characters' names: Basilius ('ruler'); Gynecia ('womanly'); Euarchus ('good ruler'); Pamela ('sweetness'); Philoclea ('lover of glory'); Pyrocles ('fire and glory'); Musidorus ('gift of the Muses'). As the translations suggest, identities in the *Old Arcadia* are linked more to character traits and offices than to individual personalities. In fact it is difficult to speak for long about Sidneian characterization without lapsing into discussion of his employment of allegory and character types. Even though we can identify passages attempting to demonstrate the workings of a mind (as in Pyrocles's dawning realization that he is in love or Basilius's anxious attempts to escape from beside his sleeping wife (*OA* 11, 197–8), it would be inappropriate to project the same sense of coherent identity that we would expect in realist novels. Sidney presents a number of positive female models for his immediate audience, and both versions of *Arcadia* constitute something of a defence of women against negative contemporary representations of perceived feminine qualities, as they demonstrate that both sexes are susceptible to being ruled by passion.[5] Sidney's characters represent models of positive and negative conduct, opportunities both for dramatizing exemplary qualities revealed through action and dialogue and for assuming particular positions in disputations. He seldom resorts to the abstract allegorical characterization seen in Spenser's Error or John Bunyan's Christian, but is interested in fashioning a narrative that provides what he calls in the *Defence* the 'imaginative groundplot' for exploring the philosophical, aesthetic and political issues with which he is concerned. 'Characters' are the means to model different aspects of these issues. As Greville describes in his *Life of Sidney* with reference to the revised *Arcadia*, though it can also be extended to the *Old*:

> [Sidney's] purpose was to limn out exact pictures of every posture in the mind that any man, being forced in the strains of this life to pass through any straits or latitudes of good or ill fortune, might (as in a glass) see how to set a good countenance upon all the discountenances of adversity, and a stay upon the exorbitant smilings of chance. (Gouws, 11)

Writing of Sidney's output as a whole Greville observes: 'in all these creatures of his making his intent and scope was to turn the barren philosophy into pregnant images of life' (Gouws, 10). In thinking about Sidney's self-conscious treatment of pastoral, the word 'pregnant' really captures that great sense of interpretative potential that Sidney's audiences are offered in works like *The Lady of May* or the *Arcadias*, how the author creates images that promise to reward our own forms of hermeneutic nurturing.

It should be apparent by now that the *Old Arcadia* is far from 'triflingly handled' and engages with a range of serious concerns. As critics such as Blair Worden have shown, it is no longer accurate to suggest that it is a wholly lightweight, romantic piece devoid of moral and political commitment, which, due to Sidney's revisions, must be subordinated to the *New Arcadia*. From the outset the *Old Arcadia* poses a major question that is simultaneously ethical and political: what happens when private interests and desires are placed above public duties and responsibilities? This is explored from many angles, though the seminal action that prompts Sidney's enquiry is Basilius's retirement, which is soon followed by his encounter and infatuation with Pyrocles–Cleophila. Sidney portrays Basilius's inability to rule – both his kingdom and himself – by stressing his effeminate nature, promoting indeed the inherently masculinist quality of what constitutes a good, successful ruler and voicing doubts regarding Elizabeth's decisiveness and capacity to rule.[6] The struggle between reason and passion foregrounded in the second eclogues occurs throughout the *Old Arcadia* and the damaging effects of unchecked passion are also seen in the increasingly serious implications of the princes' pursuit of their respective loves. Sidney deploys a series of interconnected images associated with sleep, poison and enchantment to describe the irresponsibility and derogation of duty shown by Basilius, Gynecia and the princes during their increasing subjection to love. The imagery becomes reified in book 4, when Basilius is put to sleep, though presumed poisoned. As well as the personal sense of a deviation from the expected 'main career' of an active, virtuous individual, the princes' sojourn in Arcadia has grave implications for Princess Erona, whose own pursuit of personal desire results in her facing execution unless the princes save her (*OA* 59–64). Plangus inadvertently reminds the princes on several occasions that time is running out for Erona, though the princes are too possessed by their present desires to leave Arcadia. The public implications of the princes' relationships with Basilius's daughters and their bearing upon the royal succession throws the country into turmoil by book 4, and at their trial it is their public offences in kidnapping the princesses that Euarchus identifies as their greatest crime (*OA* 351). It might also be added, however, that as a responsible ruler Basilius *should* allow his daughters to engage in dynastic marriages to secure the succession, something that Kalander in the *New Arcadia* well knows and attempts to facilitate.

From the very first mention of Gynecia in the text, her private desires attract vehement censure, and Sidney seems particularly keen to stress the folly of an older woman pursuing a younger man. It is this example of misguided passion that offers the closest commentary on political affairs of the late 1570s concerning Elizabeth's proposed marriage to the Duc d'Anjou – events on which the 1998 movie *Elizabeth* are loosely based. Marriage to Anjou, the son of Catholic Catherine de' Medici, was part of an attempt to form an alliance against Spanish aggression against the Netherlands and English mainland and was generally supported by many parties at court. By maintaining political dialogue with France, centred on the possibility of marriage, Elizabeth could protect English interests while simultaneously avoiding military intervention of the kind Leicester advocated. Anjou's notoriously vacillatory religious and political sympathies aroused fierce opposition from militant Protestants like Leicester and Sidney during the concerted suit of 1578–81. The match prompted scathing textual attacks, including John Stubbs's *A Gaping Gulfe* (1579) and Spenser's satirical beast-fable *Mother Hubberds Tale*. Sidney wrote to Elizabeth in 1579 arguing that her reign's integrity was based on maintaining the status quo: 'What makes you in such a calm to change course? To so healthful a body, to apply such a weary medicine? What hope can recompense so hazardous an adventure?' (*MP* 219). Philanax uses similar arguments to counsel Basilius against retirement. It used to be thought that royal displeasure at the letter prompted Sidney's absence from court during the period in which he completes the *Old Arcadia*, though his correspondence with Leicester reveals it was lack of money that kept him away. He may also have retreated following an altercation with the Earl of Oxford during a tennis match in August 1579. In 1581 Sidney participated in the *Four Foster Children of Desire*, an elaborate royal entertainment staging the frustration of Desire (the French suit) when confronted with the superior 'Perfect Beauty' of the queen. Sidney's concerns regarding the destructive potential of a (female) royal figure who places private interests over public good are not therefore founded simply on abstract political speculation. The Anjou match clearly informs the central line of enquiry pursued in the *Old Arcadia*.

The word 'rebellion' conjoins the private and public, personal and political dimensions of the *Old Arcadia*, playing on the analogy central to Plato's *Republic* that reason must rule desires in an individual just as a prince rules the commons in the state.[7] Obviously there are the political rebellions (resulting from personal rebellion) initiated by the Phagonians and by the populace at large following Basilius's 'death'. But rebellion is also used to describe the influence of love on Pyrocles's reason in his initial debate with Musidorus, to characterize the response Geron urges Philisides to take to 'this tyrant love' (*OA* 65), and informs imagery Pyrocles uses to describe his own overthrow in committing suicide (*OA* 255). Musidorus's internal rebellion as he succumbs to the 'overmastery' of his desires and moves to rape Pamela immediately becomes externalized when he is interrupted by the remnant of the rebels (*OA* 177). Sidney's diction repeatedly reminds us of the impact of an individual's actions upon the successful workings of state. But whilst the Phagonian rebels are clearly characterized as an abhorrent, bestial mob, aristocratic figures who defy authority in Arcadia, including the princes and princesses, are treated far more ambiguously by Sidney and ultimately escape punishment. Sidney thus forces us to assess exactly who constitute rebels in Arcadia and question in what circumstances rebellion could be considered justified. The issue is complicated further in the *New Arcadia* when during the civil war between the Laconian gentlemen and peasantry (called 'Helots') the latter are described as an oppressed force 'desirous of liberty' (*NA* 96) and Sidney remains equivocal about the justice of each side's cause.

So to whom was Sidney's critique ultimately directed? Who was the *Old Arcadia* for? The immediate answer is found in the dedication and narratorial apostrophes to Mary, who would certainly not have missed the emphasis on political themes. The text almost certainly circulated amongst those with shared literary and ideological interests: friends, many of whom were amongst the Elizabethan ruling classes, 'who will weigh errors in the balance of goodwill'. But it was never intended to influence Elizabeth herself. In the absence of detailed knowledge about how the earliest audiences responded, or on Sidney's intentions for the *New Arcadia* should it have ever been completed, we can only really treat the *Old Arcadia* as an expressive and reflective, rather than a persuasive, text. Sidney thus writes, at least partly, for himself, with the interrogative process taking place through episodes centred on disputation and interpretation. Through his writing Sidney confronts two related concerns faced in the late 1570s: the first, his dissatisfaction with what Worden calls the 'ethical inadequacy' of English and European public life; the second was Elizabeth's consistent refusal to place him in a position where he could address such failings.[8] The dedication to Mary registers anxiety that, like Basilius during his misguided retreat, Sidney occupies his leisure with pastoral entertainments and romantic adventures. But Sidney's pastoral worlds are never entirely cut off from all contact with the outside world, any more than Wilton was sealed off from the affairs and vicissitudes of court and European politics. Sidney's employment of the allusive potential of pastoral thus continually gestures beyond the realm of literal interpretation and outwards towards the context of the text's production and use. Although Sidney himself would far rather have been involved in the equivalent of rescuing Erona than listening to songs about her fate, through the ethical and political questions raised in the *Old Arcadia* he attempts to fashion an imaginative, contemplative space in which virtuous action may be interrogated, anticipated and emulated *prior* to active service itself. The text constitutes Sidney's attempt to eschew idleness, serving as a utilitarian displacement for immediate action.

3

Theory and Practice

Sidney's *Defence* is a fundamentally reactive text. It articulates Sidney's response both to the situation of writing in English in the later sixteenth century and to the emergence of his own 'unelected vocation' as a poet. C. S. Lewis famously described the mid-sixteenth century as the 'Drab' age of English poetry. After the initial promise shown by courtly makers such as Sir Thomas Wyatt and Henry Howard, the Earl of Surrey – the enduring popularity of whom is attested by multiple reprintings of that seminal anthology of early Tudor verse, Richard Tottel's *Miscellany* (1557) – English poetry advanced relatively little in sophistication or inspiration. Attempts to apply the utilitarian emphasis of early Tudor humanism to English verse resulted in stolid, overtly didactic writing, frequently deploying heavy-handed allegory to revisit traditional moral commonplaces. (This is the reason many survey courses and anthologies on Renaissance poetry leap directly from Wyatt to Sidney and concentrate on later Elizabethan literature onwards.) As Sidney himself identifies, one of the only promising mid-century works was *The Mirror for Magistrates* (first printed 1559), a popular collection of verse tragedies. Following the opening anecdote of the *Defence* describing John Pietro Pugliano's advocacy of the art of horsemanship, Sidney admits that his own area of interest is far more contentious and problematic since poetry 'from almost the highest estimation of learning is fallen to be the laughing-stock of children' (*MW* 212). As he later explains, contemporary practitioners of poetry seem to be driven more by a desire to see their work in print (and thus to subsist from their writing) than to further their knowledge of the poetic craft itself. There is little attention to the 'artificial rules' or 'imitative patterns' of poetry: to learning formal methods of poetic composition and copying models of good practice found in earlier authoritative texts (*MW* 242). The notion of a creative process characterized by conscious adherence to rules and imitation of previous writers seems anathema to our modern, post-Romantic ideas on authorial genius and originality (and the accompanying spectre of plagiarism), but for Renaissance writers and critics rules and conventions were fundamental to writing. Sidney perceives that the poor reputation of English poetry prior to 1580, when he began the *Defence*, is thus the result of a widespread failure to understand its form and function.

But things had begun to change during the 1570s, in part as English literary criticism, which was essentially formalist in nature and focused on use of rhetorical tropes and figures, caught up with the extensive, more self-conscious examination of Italian and French theorists into the purpose of imaginative writing and the validity of vernacular literature. Gascoigne's 'Notes of Instruction' concerning English verse, appended to his *Posies* collection (1575), and Sidney's experiments in quantitative verse shared with the Areopagus are some of the earliest English examples of a conscious enquiry into the form of vernacular poetry and how it might be improved. Towards the end of the *Defence* Sidney does begin to discuss the relative merits of English as a linguistic resource, continuing the discourse on English as a literary language initiated by pedagogues such as Ascham and Richard Mulcaster, though overall he deals far less with descriptive minutiae of metre or rhetorical devices. Instead, Sidney engages in a long-running debate concerning the moral utility of imaginative literature that dates back to Plato and his exclusion of poets from the model of an ideal state established in the *Republic*. Consonant with their hostile distrust of images or attraction to outward forms, Puritan reformers from the sixteenth century onwards renewed this debate as they raised similar questions concerning the value of poetry. Sidney may have undertaken the *Defence* in direct response to the latest manifestation of this controversy, the attack made on poetry in Stephen Gosson's *The School of Abuse* (1579). Gosson had addressed his text to Sidney – in search of patronage and ignorant of the latter's literary compositions – and highlighted the social threat presented by the public theatres established relatively recently in London. Controversy regarding the potential immorality of the popular stage continued well into the seventeenth century. Gosson repeatedly criticizes the way imaginative dramatic writing cannot help but inculcate idleness and effeminacy in playgoers. Regardless of whether Gosson's critique was the immediate stimulus for the *Defence*, anxieties about the related issues of idleness, effeminacy and immorality dominate the language and argument of Sidney's treatise. Indeed, he identifies the relatively peaceful stability of Elizabeth's reign as first cause of English failings in the art of poetry: 'For heretofore poets have in England also flourished, and, which is to be noted, even in those times when the trumpet of Mars did sound loudest' (*MW* 241). Sidney comments extensively on personal and political inactivity and idleness in *The Lady of May* and the *Arcadias*. Similarly, the active, martial commitment of the poet-figure forms a central strand of Sidney's argument in the *Defence* as he endeavours to demonstrate that his own literary pursuits do not disqualify him from public affairs, and indeed that writing and reading are preparatory to action.

The *Defence* is not simply a discursive essay on poetry – and for Sidney and the present discussion 'poetry' means imaginative writing as a whole – but a carefully constructed argument presented in response to the customary accusations of *mysomousoi* ('poet-haters') that poetry is worthless, deceitful and potentially corrupting. The *Defence* thus adopts a judicial tone and establishes from the outset a scenario whereby Sidney presents his case to an implied audience sitting in judgement. Identifying this scenario helps us to make sense of how the text is written and organized. It has long been noted that the *Defence* is structured according to models found in classical authorities on oratory, such as Cicero and Quintilian, and later developed in vernacular works such as Wilson's *Arte of Rhetoric*. The argument breaks down into eight parts:

1. *Exordium* (introduction) – opening anecdote about Pugliano and horsemanship that provides occasion for Sidney to defend his own 'vocation' of poetry (*MW* 212).
2. *Narratio* (outlines facts about the subject matter) – statements on the poet as prophet (*vates*) and as maker (*poiein*), and the superiority of artistry over nature (*MW* 212–17).
3. *Propositio* (the central thesis) – poetry is 'an art of imitation' (*MW* 217).

4. *Divisio* (division of argument into parts for discussion) – three kinds of poetry, eight 'parts' or genres (*MW* 217–19).
5. *Confirmatio* (evidence providing proof) – the superiority of poetry over philosophy and history as a means of moving individuals to virtuous action, and the value of different genres (*MW* 219–32).
6. *Refutatio* (refutation of opposing arguments) – refutes four specific charges against poetry, including Plato's (*MW* 232–40).
7. *Digressio* (digression, which is here structured as a mini-oration in itself) – the state of English poetry, its perceived failure to lead men to virtue, comments on drama, lyric poetry and English versification (*MW* 240–49).
8. *Peroratio* (conclusion) – sums up entire argument (*MW* 249–50).

We have already identified the centrality of formal disputations and orations in the *Old Arcadia* and seen how Sidney uses rhetorical occasions as a means of interrogation. Philanax's opening plea to Basilius, for example, adopts a similar structure to the oratical model set out above. But Sidney's mode of argument avoids the severity or rigidity of a pedagogical manual and his text overall has an elegance and clarity of exposition that is learned though personable. Sidney's tone of voice in the *Defence* can be insistent at times, even bullying, but it is also notable for its great sense of humour, as in the delightful caricatures of the moral philosopher and historian, or the impatience with opponents' arguments Sidney expresses when recounting the imputations made against poetry. Sidney wastes no time in asserting the virtue of poetry, and his *narratio*, whilst ostensibly simply providing an account of his subject, establishes much of the groundwork for the later *refutatio*, following Quintilian's directive that a *narratio* should provide a statement of facts specifically 'adapted to persuade'. When Sidney says effectively 'let me tell you what poetry is', his definitions and descriptions are carefully geared towards highlighting the inherent capacity of poets to inculcate virtuous action, how 'it is that feigning notable images of virtues, vices, or what else, with that delightful teaching' which makes a poet (*MW* 219). Similarly, the seemingly digressive excursus on the state of

English poetry serves to justify the preceding defence by demonstrating how current examples fail to achieve the *ideal* of poetry established throughout the *Defence* rather than represent an inherent failure of poetry itself.

The *Defence*'s syntax and prose style are generally less demanding for a modern readership than those of the *Arcadias*, in part due to the expository economy of Sidney's argument. One still encounters copious quotations and references to classical, Christian and contemporary sources which may look like ostentatious name-dropping, but represent Sidney's consistent recourse to illustrative examples to support his case. The opening praise of poetry as a civilizing force, citing examples from Homer to Chaucer, is typical of Sidney's syncretism of authorities and traditions. He incorporates many traditional arguments regarding poetry's origins, virtues and failings that were long-established in classical and Renaissance literary theory. Richard Willis's Latin *De re poetica disputatio* ('Disputation On Poetry') (1573) employed an oratical form to address and defend poetry using Aristotelian ideas on imitation later deployed by Sidney. But the *Defence*'s originality resides in its ability to bring together different, seemingly incompatible literary and aesthetic traditions: Neoplatonic, Aristotelian, Horatian, Ciceronian. Sidney was also familiar with contemporary Italian criticism by Tasso, Cristoforo Landino and Antonio Minturno. Of course syncretism does not necessarily imply harmony, and some of the most frequently revisited topics of criticism on the *Defence* are the perceived tensions and contradictions in Sidney's argument.

Sidney's defence of poetry begins with a qualification of the concept of the poet himself. Although professing at one point to 'speak of the art and not of the artificer' (*MW* 225), citing positive general qualities to avoid potentially negative particular examples, Sidney's term 'vocation' that initiates his argument indicates how he views the intense relationship between practice and practitioner. He is unconcerned with the profession of poet but does seek to reassert the authority of the poet-figure through demonstrating their capacity to move a reader to virtuous action. The word 'author' itself derives from Latin *auctoritas* ('authority') and this is the sense in which it was used in medieval literary and exegetical theory. Whilst Sidney never describes the poet as an 'author', his treatise contributes to the complex process whereby the modern conception of authorship begins to emerge during the sixteenth century. He also invokes the traditional idea used by ancient and modern writers alike that poetry (including printed works) offers a form of immortality both to poets and their subjects. Sidney concludes the *Defence* by conjuring his readers to recognize the value of poets and poetry or else face obscurity when they die 'for want of an epitaph' (*MW* 250).

Sidney identifies two models of poetic creativity: the poet as prophet (from Latin *vates*), and as 'maker' or artificer (from Greek *poiein*). Derived from the latter etymology, 'poem' thus signifies something that is fashioned or made. The equivalent word derived from Latin is 'fiction' but for Sidney and his peers the term encompassed both true and untrue (or 'made-up') compositions. Divinely inspired poetry – the notion that poets serve as conduits for greater metaphysical sources – is dwelt upon briefly to illustrate the incontestable virtue of David's 'heavenly poesy', the Psalms. But Sidney consistently discounts vatic poetry in order to make far greater claims for the poet's individual creative agency. Unlike practitioners of disciplines like geometry, natural philosophy or logic, which can only measure or describe extant works of nature, the poet 'doth grow in effect another nature, in making things either better than nature bringeth forth, or, quite anew, forms such as never were in nature, as the Heroes, Demigods, Cyclops, Chimeras, Furies, and such like' (*MW* 216). The poet can deliver a 'golden world', whereas nature's world is 'brazen': of brass, a more inferior metal. Sidney's assertion of the poet's god-like power to create another world echoes that made by the Frenchman Julius Caesar Scaliger, whose 1561 *Poetices libri septem* ('Seven Books on Poetics') is cited several times in the *Defence*. Scaliger drew upon over fifty years of debate amongst Italian critics that had developed around Aristotle's *Poetics*. Giorgio Valla published a Latin translation of the *Poetics* in 1498 and subsequent editions accumulated extensive commentaries occasioning detailed deliberation on genre.

Sidney's argument proceeds to modulate between the construction of an ideal and its realization within the temporal world, and between aesthetic theories espoused by Plato and

Aristotle. In perhaps the densest part of the *Defence*'s argument Sidney sets out his central definition or *propositio*: 'Poesy therefore is an art of imitation, for so Aristotle termeth it in the word *mimesis* – that is to say, a representing, counterfeiting, or figuring forth – to speak metaphorically, a speaking picture – with this end, to teach and delight' (*MW* 217). Plato had maintained that the world we live in is a flawed imitation of a perfect world of 'Ideas' or forms. Artistic representation in our world is therefore merely an imitation of an imitation. Aristotle, however, rebutted Plato by arguing that imitation is a far more creative act whereby an artist can represent things that *could* exist, and is restricted only by the limits of credibility and verisimilitude, not by whether or not something exists in our world. Therefore when Sidney a few lines earlier distinguishes the '*idea* or fore-conceit' of a work – the idea in the poet's mind that guides their creative process – from the work itself, he means that a poet forms an idea which is then imitated and expressed through the poet's act of 'representing, counterfeiting, or figuring forth'.[1] Moreover, the representation of something in the poet's work induces re-presentation in or by the reader. The proof of a poet's skill lies in the ability of the work to encourage emulation by the reader: 'not only to make a Cyrus, which had been but a particular excellency as nature might have done, but to bestow a Cyrus upon the world to make many Cyruses' (*MW* 217). Poetry for Sidney is an inherently dialogic form that relies as much upon application by the reader as it does upon the exercise of the poet's skill; it is a fundamentally user-oriented conception of poetics.

We can now return to Sidney's *propositio* to consider how poetry can fulfil its dual objectives 'to teach and delight', as propounded in Horace's *Art of Poetry*. In book 10 of the *Republic* Plato admitted that poetry might be defended successfully if 'her' advocates demonstrated that 'she is not only delightful but beneficial to orderly government and all the life of man'.[2] Sidney pursues this line at length and it forms the basis of his argument. In 1578, writing to Languet, he certainly did not believe in learning and writing simply for its own sake: 'to what purpose should our thoughts be directed to various kinds of knowledge unless room be afforded for putting it into practice so that public advantage may be the result? – which in a corrupt age we cannot hope for'.³ Such sentiments inform Musidorus's conception of the princes' learning (*OA* 12–13). Sidney's prioritization of applied knowledge was also recognized by Greville: 'But the truth is, his end was not writing even while he wrote, nor his knowledge moulded for tables or schools, but both his wit and understanding bent upon his heart to himself and others, not in words or opinion, but in life and action, good and great' (Gouws, 12). Before setting out his evidence in poetry's defence Sidney establishes his assessment criteria by identifying that all learning is directed 'to the highest end of the mistress-knowledge, by the Greeks called *architektonike*, which stands (as I think) in the knowledge of a man's self, in the ethic and politic consideration, with the end of well-doing and not of well-knowing only' (*MW* 219). Knowledge for its own sake (*gnosis*) is subordinated to practical application (*praxis*). Sidney then proceeds to demonstrate how poetry more than any other discipline can achieve this end. The association of poetry and *praxis* underlies every definition or subdivision employed in the *divisio* and *confirmatio*. Sidney initially divides poetry into three kinds: divine, philosophical and mimetic poetry proper, though he clearly favours practitioners of the third, which 'do imitate to teach and delight, and to imitate borrow nothing of what is, hath been, or shall be' (*MW* 218). Similarly, the survey of genres or 'kinds' is organized in ascending order of their ability to teach and move one to virtue, culminating with heroic poetry.

Poetry is shown to have the greatest capacity to move one to emulation when set against moral philosophy and history. Whilst philosophy teaches abstract precepts and rules and history is tied to the facts of what is or was (for example, you cannot write an account of Agincourt in which the French defeat the English), poetry can combine the didactic strengths of both. Repeatedly invoking visual metaphors, Sidney argues that the poet possesses what he later calls 'forcibleness or *energia*' by appealing directly to the reader's mind, whereas the philosopher 'bestoweth but a wordish description' (*MW* 221–2). Sir Thomas More's *Utopia* is used to illustrate how construction of a feigned commonwealth offers a more effective means of counsel than an exposition of precepts alone. Sidney uses a similar technique (called *topothesia*) when constructing his Arcadian world. Poetry is also a better teacher than history because it is not 'captived to the truth of a foolish world' in which vice often triumphs and the virtuous suffer (*MW* 225).

But the very capacity of poetry to delight and move a reader that made it the greatest teaching instrument also made it dangerous. This troubled critics such as Gosson, who saw the manipulation of the senses that occurs during one's engagement with imaginative writing as an overpowering of the reason, and consequently a threat to virtue. Sidney himself recognizes such anxieties when observing that through poetry's 'sweet charming force, it can do more hurt than any other army of words' (*MW* 236). Sidney's imagery in the *Defence* associating poetry with enchantment (which also appears in the *Republic*) invites comparison with similar schemes identified in the *Arcadias* that are linked with idleness and distraction from public duty. Ultimately the onus is placed upon the reader to distinguish between correct and incorrect usage, and Sidney stresses in the *Defence* that abuse of poetry should not invalidate poetry as a whole. Early modern concerns regarding the power of texts to influence a reader or move an audience may seem hard to appreciate nowadays, but are in fact frequently echoed in modern reservations about violence and sex in television programmes or movies.

Sidney attempts to confront potential objections from ardent Protestant critics by making the very highest claims for poetry and situating the didactic function of imaginative writing within a religious, specifically salvational context. His associations with the militant Protestant faction were discussed earlier, but several critics have demonstrated how this active Protestant commitment also extended to his conception of poetry. The claim that, due to the 'first fall of accursed Adam ... our erected wit maketh us know what perfection is, and yet our infected will keepeth us from reaching unto it' (*MW* 217) clearly adopts terms used by the reformer John Calvin, whose *Institutes of the Christian Religion* (first printed 1536) underpinned mainstream Elizabethan Protestantism. Calvin maintained that, following the fall of mankind, humanity lay in a state of wretchedness and was entirely dependent on God's grace to achieve salvation; outward works are essentially ineffectual. Some critics identify this world-view within Sidney's *Arcadia*. For example, Basilius's superstitious resort to oracles and attempt to escape his preordained fate or the workings of providence are revealed to be fruitless folly and he is duly taught a lesson through the misadventures that befall his family and kingdom.[4] Calvinist ideas of corruption and stasis were, however, directly opposed to another of the defining intellectual and philosophical currents of the Renaissance, humanism, which celebrated the human capacity to improve through the exercise of reason. Calvin divided the soul between the wit (or intellect) and the will, observing that although the latter was corrupt through its fallen nature, the former may have the capacity to investigate 'superior' (i.e. divine) objects.[5] A Calvinist or Protestant conception of poetics might exploit this distinction and identify the ability of imaginative writing to lead humanity to perceive our distance from divine perfection and recognize our reliance upon God alone. Furthermore, through attempting to gain a greater understanding of God we can begin to improve our fallen condition, a point later reiterated in works on knowledge and education by Francis Bacon and John Milton. Sidney provides one of the definitive statements of Protestant humanism in asserting that the final end of all learning 'is to lead us to as high a perfection as our degenerate souls, made worse by their clayey lodgings, can be capable of' (*MW* 219). This may seem at odds with Sidney's more human-centred *'architektonike'* identified above. But Sidney characterizes the relationship between the wit and will as one of struggle, and numerous episodes and scenarios throughout his writings re-examine the tension between perfected ideals and corrupted reality.

By the time Sidney reaches the *refutatio* and the showdown with 'poet-whippers' such as Plato, much of the work has already been done. Sidney makes continual recourse to the central statement regarding imitation and *praxis* as he addresses four criticisms raised against poetry. Against the accusation that there are many other more fruitful disciplines than poetry, he replies simply that the greatest end of learning is to inculcate virtue and, as demonstrated earlier, nothing achieves that end as successfully as poetry. Secondly, poetry has been called the 'mother of lies', though Sidney cleverly evades the charge by avowing that the poet 'nothing affirms, and therefore never lieth. For as I take it, to lie is to affirm that to be true which is false' (*MW* 235). Again, the onus is partly on the reader: is the poet to be accused of deceit if we open the *Old Arcadia* and believe there really was a Duke Basilius? To the accusation that poetry 'abuseth men's wit, training it to wanton sinfulness and lustful love' (*MW* 236), Sidney responds by revisiting the principle that abuse of a thing need not invalidate the thing itself; then cites copious illustrations of poetry's virtuous application. The authority of Plato's hostility towards poets is undermined using a similar technique. Sidney addresses one of Plato's criticisms – that contemporary poets 'filled the world with wrong opinions of the gods' – in order to show not only that this is a defunct argument within a Christian world-view but that Plato banishes 'the abuse, not the thing' (*MW* 239). Sidney ignores other elements of Plato's argument linked with deceit and degeneration, preferring to criticize the effeminacy of the philosopher's model commonwealth and what he calls the 'abominable filthiness' of practices relating to homosexuality often found in classical writings.

The gender-oriented language of both Sidney's exposition of accusations against poetry ('mother of lies', 'nurse of abuse') and his attack on Plato is a reminder of wider anxieties expressed throughout the *Defence* regarding the perceived effeminizing effects of poetry. Obviously there is an attendant personal dimension here. Sidney confronts concerns that his own 'vocation' may be effeminizing by constructing the poet as a masculinist figure. Virtuous action is characterized specifically as martial action and directly set against the potential idleness of peacetime. Heroic poetry (by which Sidney appears to signify works traditionally defined both as epic and romance) offers the most worthy models for emulation and there are many examples given of the inspirational qualities of works like *Amadis* or 'the old song of Percy and Douglas'. Observe also the many military metaphors used throughout the *Defence* to describe Sidney's discipline. The production and use of poetry are located in the active world of soldiery rather than that of the court or schoolroom: 'For poetry is the companion of camps. I dare undertake, Orlando Furioso, or honest King Arthur, will never displease a soldier' (*MW* 237). Parallel to the attempts of Italian literary critics to legitimize and moralize chivalric romance, Sidney continues to rehabilitate the form by stressing how it encourages martial valour, and accords it the same status as epic by classifying both forms under the heading of 'heroic poetry'. His attempt to synthesize the two forms continues in the *New Arcadia*.

Sidney reveals a similar form of constructive (or reconstructive) criticism when discussing drama. Critics often utilize Sidney's prescriptive comments regarding the failure of contemporary stage-plays to conform to genre decorum or Aristotelian unities (using the example of Thomas Sackville and Thomas Norton's *Gorboduc*) to situate him in a critical position identical to that of Gosson. Sidney is indeed unimpressed by the kind of metonymic expedience of the stage that later occasioned apologies from Shakespeare's Chorus in *Henry V*, whereby 'two armies fly in, represented with four swords and bucklers: and then what hard heart will not receive it for a pitched field?' (*MW* 243). No doubt the *mise en scène* of the Whitehall tiltyard was far more impressive. But Sidney is certainly not averse to using theatrical conceits, which are found throughout his writings, and it is important to note that he does not reject drama outright, even if contemporary examples are judged 'unworthy'. If structured according to the rules of unity of place and time found in classical drama, tragedy and comedy could be made far more effective and achieve 'the very end of poesy', to delightfully teach, of which it is clearly capable. The religious tragedies of Protestant scholar George Buchanan are cited as a successful example. Sidney's willingness to work with and improve debased forms is also seen in his comments on the 'bastard poets' whose 'disgraceful' poetry dominated the trade in published books. Far from unequivocally abjuring print culture because of its base practitioners, Sidney suggests that the corrective to this perceived class transgression is for gentlemen poets, who 'are better content to suppress the outflowings of their wit' than publish, to put their works into print and lead by example (*MW* 241–2). Once again it is the abuse of the thing that offends, not the thing itself. The irony is of course that Sidney publishes nothing himself and is, as Puttenham remarks, amongst that 'crew of courtly makers' whose works were rarely made public.

Oblique directions to fellow gentleman poets offer us the best glimpse of Sidney's intended audience, and the *Defence* had a very limited manuscript circulation prior to its publication in

1595. Sidney's secretary, William Temple, clearly had access to a copy when writing his *Analysis* (*c*.1584), a commentary on the *Defence* influenced by French rhetorician Petrus Ramus. Spenser may have also known the *Defence*. His letter to Raleigh that accompanied the 1590 *Faerie Queene*, declaring his intention to 'fashion a gentleman or noble person in vertuous and gentle discipline' and to moralize romance for didactic ends, reiterates many of Sidney's sentiments. There are also echoes of the *Defence* in the House of Alma episode and descriptions of Phantastes and Eumnestes (book 2, canto 9, stanzas 49–52, 55–8). In 1595 two editions of Sidney's treatise appeared in print: that published by the authorized Sidney publisher, William Ponsonby, as *The Defence of Poesy*; and a pirated version published by Henry Olney as *An Apology for Poetry*. The printed *Defence* immediately attracted wider attention, including an attempt at translating Sidney's theories into verse included by Thomas Churchyard in *A Musicall Consort of Heavenly Harmonie ... called Churchyard's Charitie* (1595).

Sidney himself could also be included among those who were influenced by the *Defence* if we believe that his special pleading for the centrality of martial virtue in romance may have prompted him to revise the *Old Arcadia*. One should be wary, however, of slavishly using the *Defence* to measure perceived Sidneian intention and identify potential successes and failings. Inconsistencies can be found within the text, regarding his attitude to vatic poetry, the role of nature, and the types of approved literature, and between the *Defence* and his letters to Robert Sidney and Sir Edward Denny, in which he advocates history over poetry. But as we have seen before, Sidney uses his writings to explore apparent contradictions, to adopt multiple positions within ongoing debates, and to register the struggle between notions of an ideal and human tendencies to deviate from the path of virtue.

4

Astrophil and Stella

By the time he began *Astrophil and Stella*, most likely during the latter part of 1581, Sidney had already experimented extensively with different variations upon the sonnet form, both in the *Old Arcadia* and the *Certain Sonnets* collection. The word 'sonnet', from Italian *sonneto* ('little sound'), is generally understood to denote a fourteen-line or 'quatorzain' lyric poem, though there are many contemporary examples that deploy more than fourteen lines, including nineteen of the *Certain Sonnets*. Comprising 108 quatorzain sonnets and eleven songs of varying length and metre Sidney's sequence charts the suit of a virtuous married woman Stella ('star') by the young, self-conscious, increasingly obsessive courtier Astrophil ('star-lover'). It adopts essentially the same narrative arc found in Sidney's Philisides–Mira poems, though Astrophil is far more physical and sexual than Philisides.

In the first, unauthorized edition of *Astrophil*, published by Thomas Newman in 1591, the preface by Nashe promised the reader a 'Theater of pleasure' and sketched out the tragic shape of Astrophil's story:

> here you shal find a paper stage strued with pearle, an artificial heau'n to ouershadow the faire frame, & christal wals to encounter your curious eyes, whiles the tragicommody of loue is performed by starlight. The chief Actor here is Melpomene [Muse of tragedy], whose dusky robes dipt in the ynke of teares, as yet seeme to drop when I view them neere. The argument cruell chastitie, the Prologue hope, the Epilogue dispaire.[1]

The first sixty or so sonnets find Astrophil engaged in a seemingly fruitless adoration and pursuit of his beloved, but then in a sequence from Sonnets 61–72 Stella offers a guarded declaration of her love for Astrophil, a chaste love that will uphold her virtue:

> She in whose eyes love, though unfelt, doth shine,
> Sweet said that I true love in her should find.
> I joyed, but straight thus watered was my wine,
> That love she did, but loved a love not blind,
> Which would not let me, whom she loved, decline
> From nobler course, fit for my birth and mind:
> And therefore, by her love's authority,
> Willed me these tempests of vain love to fly,
> And anchor fast myself on virtue's shore.
>
> (Sonnet 62)

Astrophil is elated and imagines the physical pleasures to come, as revealed in Song 1. There then follows an intensification of Astrophil's struggle to control his physical desire for Stella and subordinate his passions to reason. Despite professions in Sonnets 5 and 25 to maintain an idealized, Neoplatonic, non-sexual love founded on an attraction to virtue, the niceties of chaste 'courtly love' are not enough for Astrophil's charged sexual passions and he snatches a kiss in Song 2, though is quickly rebuked and spurned. Subsequent songs reiterate Stella's conception of virtuous love, emphasizing that in order to maintain her honourable reputation she must reject the kind of physical love and consummation Astrophil clearly desires:

> Trust me, while I thee deny,
> In my self the smart I try;
> Tyrant honour thus doth use thee;
> Stella's self might not refuse thee.
>
> (Song 8, ll. 93–6)

The remainder of the sequence sees Astrophil wrestling with the frustrations and limitations of his situation, still evidently absorbed with the process of externalizing his inner torment though momentarily shifting between realization of his folly and desire to abandon his suit (as in Sonnet 107), and despair that an escape from this situation and its expressive framework may prove impossible (Sonnet 108).

Modern readers unaccustomed to sonnet sequences often encounter difficulties with the way that a story is told over a series of individual poems, rightly observing that the structure does not seem as straightforward as more linear narrative poetry like, say, Shakespeare's *Venus and Adonis*. Although *Astrophil* was probably written over a relatively short period of time, the multipart nature of sonnet sequences could allow for earlier pieces, previously independently composed, to be integrated into the new structure. It is necessary to realize that the individual poems are what Maurice Evans calls the 'by-product' of an implied narrative concerning Astrophil's pursuit of Stella.[2] Rather than looking for the 'real' story behind the poems, we should read each sonnet as representing individual high or low points in an extra-textual affair, which are organized together with the same coherence as a collection of photographs in an album. They are occasions for contemplation and articulation, rather than action, and for exploring a situation through a particular intellectual or emblematic formulation. See, for example, Sonnet 31, where Astrophil speculates on the constancy of lunar and sublunary love, or Sonnet 84, addressed to the highway to his beloved's house, where Astrophil literally worships the ground on which Stella walks. *Astrophil*'s presentation is further complicated by the complex temporal position and narratorial standpoint of the 'I'-speaker. The poems are simultaneously *of* and *about* praise (as is played on in Sonnet 35); they provide both the account of the affair and the instrument of seduction.[3] At times Astrophil addresses a friend about an ongoing amatory process, at others the sonnets appear as torch-songs for a now-lost love.

Sidney's sequence clearly draws upon the story structure and narrative conventions established by Petrarch's archetypal tale of unrequited passion set out in his *Rime Sparse* ('Scattered Poems'), composed 1327–74. Whilst Petrarch did not invent the sonnet itself, he was one of the first to assemble a collection of sonnets, together with longer songs (*canzone*), in order to anatomize his adoration for a woman he had seen and idealized (who was probably unaware of Petrarch's attention), his beloved Laura. In doing so Petrarch establishes a representational mode for articulating every facet of the pleasure and pain of being in love, which was to dominate European lyric poetry for over three centuries. Petrarch's great innovation was to use the sonnet to emphasize interiority, the intellectual and emotional effects of the lover's frustrated suit upon a construction of his sense of self. Petrarch fashions an expression of selfhood through use of a first-person 'I'-figure in order to explore both earthly and heavenly love. In particular he emphasizes the shifting instability of the lover's self and the divisions and contradictions caused by his desire. This is reflected on numerous occasions in the structure of individual sonnets. Within the economy of fourteen lines Petrarch relates the movement of his thought-process to the rhyme scheme's deployment. The Petrarchan sonnet is distinguished by a marked division between the first eight lines, the octave, and the remaining six, the sestet, typically rhyming ABBAABBA CDECDE. The turning point or *volta* between octave and sestet could be used to juxtapose contradictory thoughts or lines of enquiry, or to raise and resolve points of doubt. In Petrarch's hands the sonnet becomes a concise expressive mechanism for registering and exploring anxieties of the self, in the first instance relating to love.

Both the form and expressive mode of Petrarch's sonnets were introduced into early modern English poetry through the translations and adaptations of the *Rime Sparse* made by Wyatt and Surrey at Henry VIII's court. Puttenham does not exaggerate when he writes

> In the latter end of the same king's reign sprong up a new company of courtly makers, of whom Sir Thomas Wyatt the elder and Henry, Earl of Surrey were the two chieftains, who having travelled into Italy, and there tasted the sweet and stately measures and style of the Italian poesy, as novices newly crept out of the schools of Dante, Ariosto and Petrarch, they greatly polished our rude and homely manner of vulgar poesy from that it had been before, and for that cause may justly be said the first reformers of our English metre and style.[4]

The Henrician poets' 'Englishing' of Petrarch had a huge influence upon the tone and direction of English poetry throughout the sixteenth century, and their works – which were never structured into sequences – would have been known to Sidney's generation through Tottel's *Miscellany*. But the ongoing 'translation' process was far more creative than simple, slavish importation of phrasing and imagery. Like Wyatt and Surrey and several of his own contemporaries, Sidney proceeded to make Petrarchan conventions his own through a fundamental practice of humanist pedagogy and rhetoric known as *imitatio*: using the Italian's poetry as an authoritative model, copying or imitating individual features and then incorporating these into his own compositions. Again this seems at odds with modern ideas about creativity and originality, and indeed Sidney himself periodically expresses grave reservations about such practice in *Astrophil* (e.g. Sonnet 1). Perhaps the closest analogy to *imitatio* in twenty-first-century creative composition is the practice of 'sampling' and re-mixing in modern dance music.

Astrophil is not the first English sonnet sequence. The Calvinist Anne Locke appended a short sequence to a translation of one of Calvin's sermons in 1560 and in 1582 Thomas Watson published *Hekatompathia*, a rather scholarly series of a hundred eighteen-line sonnets which included a prose précis explaining the conceits used. So what makes *Astrophil* so original and, consequently, influential? In part it is Sidney's creation of the character of Astrophil himself, who comes across as an energetic, clearly drawn personality riddled with doubts and anxieties, whose persistent preoccupation, as much with his wooing of Stella (and how to express this) as with Stella herself, forms the implicit point of contiguity between all the poems in the sequence. It is the central courtship narrative that provides the sequence's common binding structure in a similar manner to Petrarch's focus on Laura; thus *Astrophil* can be rightly considered the first English Petrarchan sonnet sequence.

Our attraction as readers to the compelling implied drama of the self-obsessed Astrophil has been compared to the continued fascination – for audiences and critics alike – with Hamlet's character, as we revisit the internal conflicts that they themselves fail to resolve. The sense of drama or possibly melodrama created in *Astrophil* and identified by Nashe is another particularly Sidneian feature. Astrophil's voice repeatedly evokes dramatic scenarios in which he invites an implied audience to witness a particular image or event, as in Sonnet 20 ('Fly, fly, my friends, I have my death wound, fly'), or where he appears to muster some resolve and autonomy – until he sees Stella:

> What, have I thus betrayed my liberty?
> Can those black beams such burning marks engrave
> In my free side? or am I born a slave,
> Whose neck becomes such yoke of tyranny?
> Or want I sense to feel my misery?
> Or spirit, disdain of such disdain to have,

> Who for long faith, though daily help I crave,
> May get no alms, but scorn of beggary?
> Virtue, awake; beauty but beauty is;
> I may, I must, I can, I will, I do
> Leave following that, which it is gain to miss.
> Let her go. Soft, but here she comes. Go to,
> Unkind, I love you not – : O me, that eye
> Doth make my heart give to my tongue the lie.
>
> (Sonnet 47)

Sometimes there is a dramatic nature to his internal debates:

> Come let me write. 'And to what end?' To ease
> A burdened heart. 'How can words ease, which are
> The glasses [mirrors] of thy daily vexing care?'
> Oft cruel fights well pictured forth do please.
> 'Art not ashamed to publish thy disease?'
> Nay, that may breed my fame, it is so rare.
> 'But will not wise men think thy words fond ware?'
> Then be they close, and so none shall displease.
> 'What idler thing, than speak and not be heard?'
> What harder thing than smart, and not to speak?
> Peace, foolish wit; with wit my wit is marred.
> Thus write I while I doubt to write, and wreak
> My harms on ink's poor loss; perhaps some find
> Stella's great powers, that so confuse my mind.
>
> (Sonnet 34)

Both excerpted examples demonstrate Sidney's level of fluency and dexterity with the sonnet form. While there are points where Astrophil adopts a declamatory voice or makes apostrophic addresses to his audience or to abstract concepts – such as virtue (Sonnet 4), sleep (Sonnet 39), hope (Sonnet 67), grief (Sonnet 94) – the overall tone is conversational and closer to the rhythms of speech. Earlier sonneteers tend to use each sonnet line as the basic organizational unit for a clause or sentence, but Sidney repeatedly uses enjambement to extend a thought or phrase across multiple lines.

Sidney's mastery of the form is also evident in his relation of thought-process and argument to the sonnets' structure. Sidney employs a number of variations upon the sonnet form pioneered by Surrey, which was divided into three quatrains and a concluding couplet and which largely became standard for

Elizabethan sonnets. Such a form (the 'English sonnet') offered Sidney a greater range of expressive options than the Italian form with its single *volta* as there are up to four distinct units through which to develop or cross-examine an idea or conceit, to modify the direction of an argument or to heighten its intensity, as he does so successfully in Sonnet 101. In particular the final couplet could be used to provide an epigrammatic reflection upon or epitome of the argument of the preceding twelve lines, and Sidney frequently exploits the histrionic potential of the build-up to the couplet. Equally the couplet can undercut and contradict what has just been established. In Sonnet 72 Astrophil spends twelve lines building up to the abandonment of his worldly desires only to experience a moment of doubt in the final lines: 'But thou, desire, because thou would'st have all,/ Now banished art – but yet, alas, how shall?' Similarly, in Sonnet 18 Astrophil is 'audited' by Reason and finds himself bankrupt 'Of all those goods, which heaven to me hath lent' and argues with himself that his wit should rule his passions. Yet even though he perceives his potentially self-destructive trajectory, 'I see, and yet no greater sorrow take/ Than that I lose no more for Stella's sake'. Sidney returns here to the familiar struggle between erected wit and infected will and again considers the place of his writings therein, in this case fearing his youth has been 'idly spent' on amorous 'toys'.

Petrarch's influence was not restricted to form and *Astrophil* exhibits Sidney's studied familiarity with the conventional vocabulary, imagery and *topoi* of the *Rime Sparse* and its later continental and English distillates. Petrarch synthesized the playful cult of Cupid from classical poetry and the subtle eroticism of the biblical Song of Songs, with the notion developed in medieval troubadour poetry that being in love involved an intense, often arduous form of service to the beloved. Petrarch strove to provide a verbal representation of a cerebral response to an emotional state and made frequent use of oxymoron, conceits and hyperbolic physical description in an attempt to comprehend the paradoxical condition of being in love; how can something as wonderful as love cause so much pain? Sidney often plays upon such conventions:

> Some lovers speak, when they their muses entertain,
> Of hopes begot by fear, of wot not what desires,

Of force of heavenly beams, infusing hellish pain,
Of living deaths, dear wounds, fair storms and freezing fires.

(Sonnet 6)

Sidney's representation of Stella frequently evokes the stylized descriptions of female beauty used in the Petrarchan blazon, a poetic 'check-list' of ideal physical attributes that might include golden hair, dark eyes (or eyes compared to suns or stars), rubious lips and fair skin (see Sonnets 7, 8, 9, 12, 77, 91, Song 1). Sidney offers one of the finest examples of the blazon in Philisides's 'What tongue can her perfections tell', though the form became rather hackneyed by the early seventeenth century and Shakespeare parodies its conventions in his Sonnet 130, 'My mistress' eyes are nothing like the sun'.

Sidney also appropriates imagery casting love as a war or heroic struggle and subjugates the beloved under the lover's tyranny; see, for example, Sonnets 2, 20, 47, and Song 5. The concept of gaining 'governance' over Stella, if only momentarily, is expressed in similarly political terms when Astrophil exclaims 'For Stella hath, with words where faith doth shine,/ Of her high heart giv'n me the monarchy' (Sonnet 69). In Sonnet 49 Sidney employs the conceit of being ridden by the figure of love itself: 'I on my horse, and love on me, doth try/ Our horsemanships'. Astrophil's condition is not simply one of passive frustration; it is unequivocally a power dynamic – albeit one in which he chooses to situate himself – where he is the subject of both internal desires and external forces. Sidney's frequent use of imagery associated with poisoning, burning and enchantment or witchcraft to describe Astrophil's situation invites comparisons with similar language employed by Musidorus and Pyrocles to speak of the overpowering effects of love, and to further consider links between the language(s) of politics and desire. Of course, the great irony of the Petrarchan mode employed by Sidney is that the beloved Stella, though ostensibly in a position of power, is essentially mute and entirely recreated and expressed through Astrophil. Even where she is allowed speech in Song 8, this is modulated through the narratorial 'I'-speaker. It is therefore possible to view the sequence as a verbal means of correcting the professed power imbalance, and indeed of using a dialogic 'I–you' relationship to fashion an authoritative first-person rhetorical stance to explore far weightier issues than love, as is suggested below.

At the same time as imitating aspects of the Petrarchan tradition, Sidney remains deeply sceptical of recourse to poetic conventions, and rarely utilizes such without querying their efficacy and validity, as in Sonnet 52 which charts the strife between physical love, epitomized by an attention to Stella's body, and the spiritual virtue enshrined in her soul. One of the key dilemmas in *Astrophil* is how to represent and persuade – something Sidney finds sorely lacking in contemporary lyric poetry (*MW* 246) – but avoid coming across as overtly artificial. The opening sonnet sets the terms of the exploratory process that follows:

> Loving in truth, and fain in verse my love to show,
> That she (dear she) might take some pleasure of my pain;
> Pleasure might cause her read, reading might make her know;
> Knowledge might pity win, and pity grace obtain;
> I sought fit words to paint the blackest face of woe,
> Studying inventions fine, her wits to entertain;
> Oft turning others' leaves, to see if thence would flow
> Some fresh and fruitful showers upon my sunburnt brain.
> But words came halting forth, wanting invention's stay;
> Invention, nature's child, fled step-dame study's blows;
> And others' feet still seemed but strangers in my way.
> Thus great with child to speak, and helpless in my throes,
> Biting my truant pen, beating myself for spite,
> 'Fool', said my muse to me; 'look in your heart, and write'.
>
> (Sonnet 1)

The first quatrain models how through reading these words Stella might be stimulated to action, i.e. the provision of 'grace': reciprocated affection and, hopefully, sexual gratification. Sidney establishes a *praxis*-oriented trajectory for his sequence but then immediately questions how to proceed, apparently scornful of those who compose by imitation and initially work from words rather than the subject itself. The concluding couplet rejects artificial means of 'invention' in favour of more spontaneous, natural textual generation. The first three sonnets in *Astrophil* repeatedly criticize the kind of 'imitative patterns' that Sidney elsewhere commends in the *Defence* (*MW* 242), consciously adopting a pose of spontaneity and questioning whether one requires the Petrarchan vocabulary for sincere expression (see also Sonnets 15 and 54). *Astrophil* is therefore often called an anti-Petrarchan sequence, though attempts to apply binaries of 'pro-' and 'anti-' ultimately mask the sequence's essentially inquisitive, interrogatory, playful nature. For example, despite its denial of studied artistry Sonnet 1 is crammed with rhetorical and poetic devices: metaphorical schemes; the trope *gradatio* or connective climax (ll. 1–4); wordplay on the term for a metrical unit, 'feet'; evocation of a muse. Sidney also inaugurates his sequence with an innovation for English metre, the twelve-syllable alexandrine line. (He also uses alexandrines in Sonnets 6, 8, 76, 77 and 103.) From the outset Sidney makes continual reference to the poet's craft, and he returns to the theme frequently (see Sonnets 3, 6, 15, 18, 34–5, 58); *Astrophil* is as much – if not more – concerned with the representation of love as with love itself. Sidney interrogates his 'unelected vocation' throughout the sequence, questioning in particular the formal conventions, rhetorical stance and pragmatic application of love poetry. Sonneteers both before and after Sidney similarly evince a self-conscious awareness of the writing process within their own poems, but what really generates *Astrophil*'s originality is its overwhelming playfulness and comic execution. Although *Astrophil* does not resolve the narrator's personal dilemma, the sequence foregrounds its witty representation.[5]

Earlier generations of critics sought to interpret *Astrophil* as a veiled reflection of a romantic affair between Sidney and Penelope Devereux. Penelope came to court in 1581 and would have there met Sidney, possibly for the first time. She married Robert, Lord Rich, in November the same year. There is little doubt that Sidney uses Penelope as the model for the virtuous married woman Stella, and several sonnets allude to and scorn her husband, as in Sonnet 24, which begins 'Rich fools there be', or alternatively praise Lady Rich's name (Sonnet 37). Sidney's earliest audiences, such as Harington, were quick to make the identification, though it is impossible to gauge the exact depth of Sidney's potentially adulterous desires for Penelope. One must be cautious about how we understand the relationship between Sidney and his narrator Astrophil. Sidney does offer conscious invitations to see projections of himself in his sequence. As well as obvious onomastic echoes of the author in the name 'Astrophil', the sequence's speaker shares a number of Sidney's attributes and biographical features: he is a courtly figure with equestrian interests (Sonnet 53) whose father serves in Ireland (Sonnet 30) and who appears to have taken part in the *Four Foster Children of Desire* tournament (Sonnet 41). He also bears the Sidney coat of arms featuring an arrowhead (Sonnet 65). It would be mistaken, however, to read *Astrophil* as unmediated autobiography, an extended *roman-à-clef* of an actual relationship. (In Sonnet 28 Sidney dismisses those who read like this 'with allegory's curious frame'.) The first-person perspective of sonnet sequences can beguile one into interpreting the poems as intimate confessions of personal thoughts, emotions and events experienced by the narrator; witness the analogous biographical obsession within Shakespeare studies and attempts to identify the 'dark lady' of the sonnets. But it is very much a given of Renaissance love lyrics that the author could detach himself from the speaker of sonnets, and that the 'I'-figure was simply a narratorial and rhetorical position. As Lewis writes, 'a good sonnet is like a good public prayer; the test is whether the congregation can "join" and make it their own'.[6] Just as characters in the *Arcadias* make one another's verses their own to woo their respective beloveds, so individual poems or whole sequences could be redeployed together with their first-person narrators.

More recent critics have developed this line and examined the social and political functions of sonnets at Elizabeth's court. As Arthur Marotti has shown, sonnet sequences circulated in manuscript played a significant role within the performative courtly world where the language of love and that of politics were intricately interwoven.[7] Sidney, it is suggested, was more interested in the abstract concept of a power relationship initiated by desire than in a particular object of affection. Using the paradigmatic Petrarchan standpoint of a lover's experience of frustrated desire, Sidney could articulate his own sense of impotent service to a powerful female: the queen. Astrophil's frustrated desire is a reflection of Sidney's 'great expectations' yet very limited political and social advancement up to and around 1581–2. Aside from possible regret over Penelope's marriage, Sidney harboured disappointment when he was disinherited of Leicester's estate and titles upon the birth of the earl's son in April 1581. At the next tilt-day that year he bore the device ~~SPERAVI~~ ('I used to hope') to display his cancelled ambitions. Even Sidney's knighthood in 1583 was only awarded so that he could act as proxy to Prince Casimir when the latter was made Knight of the Garter. Sidney's sonnet sequence functions as a means of vocalizing his frustrations at a failed courtship – both political and amatory – to his immediate peers at court, including Greville and Dyer, a coterie audience implicitly addressed in the poems themselves and who communicate their experiences through their own lyrics. Several of Greville's poems in *Caelica* address questions or musings presented in *Astrophil* or imitate the language and imagery of Sidney's verse; compare, for example, Song 8 with *Caelica* 76.

Sidney's tale of frustrated desire can be abstracted a stage further to reveal analogies of the lover/beloved relationship, not only to that between suitor and patron, but between believer and God. Such a reading begins to align with the concept of a Protestant poetics advanced in the *Defence*, in particular the formulation of literary expression that drew upon realization of the human weakness and helplessness encouraged by the Calvinist mode. The Calvinist believer is continually caught in the position of realizing the need for divine grace but being frustrated from attaining it directly for themselves. We saw earlier how a characteristic feature of Sidney's writing is his anatomization of contention between earthly desires and lofty ideals and the attempt to reconcile 'infected will' and 'erected wit'. But for all the apparent tension between courtly love and Protestant piety, Petrarchanism and Protestantism share a situation and vocabulary of frustration and anxiety, and are alike in providing what Gary Waller calls 'complex mechanisms whereby the desiring subject was permitted to speak, put under observation, and articulated in the presence and under the power of an Other (a mistress or a God)'.[8] The tension between 'infected' and 'erected' human faculties remains present in, indeed animates, all of Sidney's writings, but it is one that utilizes a shared contemplative and discursive space.

It is difficult therefore to argue, as some have, that poetry wholly 'fails' at the end of *Astrophil*, or that Sidney ultimately rejects poetry, on the basis that Astrophil himself was unsuccessful in his suit and begs leave of Stella in Sonnet 107 to pursue an unspecified 'great cause, which needs both use and art'. A similar abnegatory gesture is made in the final two poems of *Certain*

Sonnets. Admittedly, a number of sonnets see Astrophil subordinating political affairs and ambition to his pursuit of Stella (e.g. Sonnets 23, 27, 30), and one of the sequence's paradoxes is its simultaneous sense of avowal and denial: an awareness of what *should* be done but is currently abandoned. Despite the martial imagery of Petrarchan love-discourse the poet of *Astrophil* does not entirely fit with the ideal warrior-poet modelled in the *Defence*. His hero abandons public life, pursues a married woman and spectacularly fails in the Neoplatonic love games expected of Castiglione's ideal courtier. But perhaps Sidney still preserves an image of virtue in the sequence through the absent presence of Stella and her refusal to acquiesce to unchaste love; *Astrophil* thus teaches as much by negative example as positive.[9] Sidney, like *Astrophil*, may have composed his sequence during a dilatory period of relative political inactivity, but it is still informed by the political dimension of what it means to 'court', by the inequitable power relationship maintained by the desire for grace or reward and the verbal means used to articulate and negotiate the situation. Sidney's self-conscious writing about the writing of love provides another perspective from which to examine the relation of active and contemplative modes. In particular, writing is repeatedly presented as a valid displacement for action, and Sonnet 34 even explores the possibility that it might function as a form of therapy. More significantly, since *Astrophil* is presented as being instrumental both in enacting and reflecting on the wooing process, it offers Sidney a working model of how writing can continue to address personal anxieties regarding political disappointment and inactivity in that it is situated *between* the active and contemplative poles. *Astrophil* does not conclude with a neat sense of resolution but it constitutes another phase of Sidney's ongoing interrogation of the social and political function of writing, and of the relative merits of different forms. *Astrophil* may not match the ideal for lyric poetry presented in the *Defence*:

> which, Lord, if He gave us so good minds, how well it might be employed, and with how heavenly fruit, both private and public, in singing the praises of the immortal beauty: the immortal goodness of that God who giveth us hands to write and wits to conceive; of which we might well want words, but never matter; of which we could turn our eyes to nothing, but we should ever have new-budding occasions. (*MW* 246)

But this does not mean that Sidney rejects poetry outright. Poems like Sonnet 18 might dismiss amatory poetry as idle 'toys', yet the closing reference to a 'great cause, which needs both use and art' (Sonnet 107) – assuming the usual caveats about autobiographical interpretations – appears to look towards artistic projects of a more virtuous strain that Stella herself requests ('what thy own will attends'), such as the revised *Arcadia* or translation of the Psalms and religious works by Guillaume du Bartas and Philippe de Mornay.

Toys or not, Sidney sonnets were highly influential. *Astrophil* circulated in manuscript during the 1580s and first appeared in print in Newman's 1591 edition, produced, says the publisher, 'because I thought it pittie anie thing proceeding from so rare a man, shoulde bee obscured'. Newman's first edition also included a selection of sonnets from Greville, Samuel Daniel and Thomas Campion, all figures connected with the Wilton circle, offering a printed sampler of coterie verse. Sidney's sister Mary secured a government order to suppress this pirated edition and forced Newman to produce a corrected edition, though a better version was included in the 1598 folio of Sidney's collected works. The publication of amatory poetry by a well-born courtier was a revolutionary moment for sixteenth-century literature – Marotti calls it a 'landmark publishing event' – as it suddenly offered a 'sociocultural legitimation' for the printed lyric.[10] Challenging notions of a stigma of print, or undermining arguments of those maintaining such existed, Sidney's printed sonnets established an authoritative precedent soon followed by writers such as Daniel, Spenser and many lesser poets. Sidney's manipulation of Petrarch encouraged others to take the sonnet in many different directions: to contrast fickle worldly love with divine constancy (Greville); to conclude an amorous sequence with consummation and marriage (Spenser); to compose a sequence from the female perspective (Lady Mary Wroth); and to use the sonnet for homoerotic praise (Shakespeare, Richard Barnfield). Several of *Astrophil*'s songs (6, 8, 9, 10, 11) were set to music and appeared in collections by William Byrd (1587), Thomas Morley (1600) and Robert Dowland (1610).

5

Refashionings

At some point between 1583 and 1584 Sidney began revising the *Old Arcadia*. By the time he abandoned the text prior to travelling to the Netherlands in November 1585, leaving the manuscript with Greville, he had made radical changes to the structure and tone of his 'toyfull book'. Although he only completed reworking two and a half of the original five books the revised material was over 50,000 words longer than the completed *Old Arcadia*. The *New Arcadia* preserves the interaction of poetry and prose found in the original but, although Sidney reorders and reassigns some of the incidental pieces, he composes few new poems for the revised version.

Even before revision begins there are suggestions of a work *like* the *New Arcadia* within the earlier version: narratorial asides promise to return at a later point to the complex back-story of Erona's capture and defer recitation of the princes' valiant acts beyond Arcadia to 'a work for a higher style than mine' (*OA* 10). Further hints of narrative material concerning events in Arcadia conclude the *Old Arcadia*, possibly alluding to an unfinished fifth set of eclogues, and suggest that somebody else tells, amongst other things, of the 'strange continuance' of Klaius and Strephon's desire (*OA* 361). Klaius and Strephon appear earlier in the fourth eclogues where Sidney declares it 'would require a whole book to recount their sorrows and the strange causes of their sorrows' and tell of their shared love for Urania (*OA* 284–5). Sidney never goes that far, but the pair do feature in perhaps the first example of a reworking of the Arcadian matter, the unfinished *Lamon's Tale*, composed around 1581. As a suggestive illustration of how further narrative threads could and would be spun out of Sidney's original story and rewoven into the *New Arcadia*, the pair reappear in the revised version's opening scene, again complaining of their mistress's absence.

Sidney makes many different kinds of changes to his original text and the *New Arcadia* represents a total transformation of both the type of story he sets out to tell and how it is told. It is no longer presented within the generic matrix of pastoral comedy but instead, from the outset, has all of the trappings of heroic romance – battles, jousts, duels and sieges – and bears a greater affinity to Sidney's Hellenistic, Spanish and Italian romance-epic sources. The generic shift is most prominent in the composite 1593 version when the martial actions of the revised book 3 are brought to a close and there is an appreciable return to a more relaxed pace and tone, albeit momentarily, given the crises of the final two books. Most of the narrative material and incidental poetry of the original is present in the *New Arcadia* as are all of the familiar set-pieces: the prophecy and retreat; the attack by the lion and bear; the love intrigues and disguisings; and the rebellion and its pacification. But this has been greatly expanded upon, reorganized and contextualized, and there are a vast number of new episodes and characters. For a start, Sidney places far greater emphasis on Musidorus and Pyrocles's numerous adventures prior to their arrival in Arcadia, with both the princes and other characters telling of plots in which they have been involved and to which they must return in the future. Distributed throughout the first two revised books is a wealth of information about the princes' multiple entanglements with the extended families of the Greek and Near-Eastern nobility and the complex dynastic struggles between Erona, her spurned suitor King Tiridates of Armenia and his vengeful sister Artaxia. No sooner do the princes escape from shipwreck at the start of the text than they find themselves on opposite sides of a civil war in Laconia, a kingdom bordering Arcadia. At every stage Sidney strives to flesh out a coherent political context for his story and present a range of different models of rule, both idealized and tyrannous. He is equally careful to situate his story within a precise and accurate geography drawn both from classical sources and the most up-to-date sixteenth-century maps.[1]

The most significant additions to the original narrative concern Basilius's sister-in-law Cecropia and her son Amphialus. The first mention of the latter comes when the Arcadian gentleman Kalander informs Musidorus of Basilius's retirement and voices his fears about the dangers presented by the 'valiant'

Amphialus (*NA* 82). The beasts that threaten the royal family in book 1 are now revealed to belong to Cecropia. Her animal-keeper was apparently unable to control them, though Gynecia suspects more sinister causes 'because she had heard much of the devilish wickedness of her [Cecropia's] heart, and that particularly she did her best to bring up her son Amphialus ... to aspire to the crown as next heir male after Basilius' (*NA* 181–2). Such fears are realized in the entirely rewritten book 3 in which Cecropia abducts Pamela, Philoclea and the disguised Pyrocles, holds them captive at her castle and mentally abuses the princesses. Meanwhile Amphialus fends off repeated assaults from Basilius's besieging army until his mother accidentally falls from a roof and dies and he in turn severely injures himself. He is eventually borne off to Helen of Corinth, never to return in the extant text.

Reading successive versions of the *Arcadias* (which is something few initial readers actually did) allows one to observe and appreciate events only previously reported in passing, such as Pyrocles's encounter with Philoclea's portrait in Kalander's (formerly Kerxenus's) house (*NA* 74) or the background to the princes' appropriation of names adopted during their disguised sojourn in Arcadia. (Musidorus adopts the name Palladius on his initial travels, before using Dorus in Arcadia; Pyrocles uses Daiphantus initially and is then called Zelmane, rather than Cleophila, once in Amazon guise.) The *New Arcadia* also reveals the narrative 'working' that lies behind well-known events in the story and Sidney's increased attention to political causation. In her first scene Cecropia reveals that she was ultimately behind the Phagonian rebellion having got her servant Clinias to fuel the multitude's fears about Basilius's absence and infatuation with Pyrocles–Zelmane. The received narrative of the rebel cause given by the narrator in the *Old Arcadia* (*OA* 111–12) and Clinias in the *New* (*NA* 389–93) thus veils Cecropia's personal, vengeful motives (*NA* 444–7). Similarly, Amphialus invokes an argument found in Huguenot political theory, concerning subaltern magistrates (in this case Philanax) that threaten royal authority, to justify the war caused by the princesses' abduction (*NA* 452–4). In reality Cecropia ordered the princesses' capture so that Amphialus could better pursue his affections for Philoclea. Credible public causes are deployed to mask more base personal desires. Sidney's renewed emphasis upon political realities and positivist causation can also be seen as another aspect of his attempt to rehabilitate the romance genre and confront those humanist critics who derided the form as meaningless, fantastic and unstructured.

One of the greatest causes of confusion for readers first encountering the *New Arcadia* is the highly convoluted way in which the story is told, particularly in books 1 and 2, through a series of flashbacks, episodes set in the 'present', and reports of 'off-stage' events. Like many great classical epics and their early modern imitations, the *New Arcadia* starts *in medias res* with the action of the story already under way. Klaius and Strephon interrupt their meditation on Urania, itself a remembrance of past events, in order to rescue Musidorus, who soon supplies extensive information about how he and Pyrocles reached where we find them at the start of the text. Whereas in the *Old Arcadia* the initial prophecy proleptically mapped out the narrative trajectory of the text, in the *New Arcadia* we hear nothing of it until towards the end of book 2 following the rebellion, when Basilius attempts to interpret its predictions according to recent events shown thus far. Prior to this a greater sense of mystery surrounds Basilius's retreat, both for Philanax and fellow Arcadians and for the reader of the revised text. As the story progresses the action is continually interrupted by shepherds and messengers running in breathlessly with news and additional tales, verbally recreating an ensemble cast of characters and leading the reader off into a labyrinth of plots and subplots, of tales within tales. Episodes set out in a linear fashion in the *Old Arcadia* are now fragmented and distributed through the expanded text. The princes' debate on love, for example, spans five chapters of book 1, and the interruption caused by Kalander's hunt momentarily defers Pyrocles's revelation to Musidorus of the object of his affections (*NA* 114). As Evans observes, Sidney again intervenes in the ongoing debate within sixteenth-century literary theory concerning the relative merits of the single plot centred on a single hero, identified by Aristotle as a characteristic generic feature of epic, and the multiple, interlace plotting employed in romance (*NA* 20–21). In practice Sidney appears to have attempted a formal synthesis consonant with contemporary Italian theorists on heroic poetry, a term he uses in the *Defence* to describe works of both epic and romance.

Management of the narrative and causal threads in the *Old Arcadia* was explicitly the responsibility of Sidney's intrusive, though genial narrator figure. The *New Arcadia*'s narration is far more impersonalized and there is little sense of a mediating character playing out the story to the 'fair ladies' of the audience and making apostrophic appeals to his readers. What narratorial commentary there is takes the form of parenthetical asides. Emphasis is placed on the story, not the storyteller, and characters themselves deliver significant amounts of introductory information.[2] Kalander now provides the opening political description of Arcadia, complete with its subtle critique of Basilius and household; Pyrocles now personally confesses how he fell in love with Philoclea (*NA* 75–9, 140–42). Again there is a more realist focus here as Sidney downplays any sense of there being an authoritative controlling narrator and demonstrates how all of the information that we receive is partial, provisional and sometimes deployed for personal gain.

Although vast in overall size, because of the numerous additions to the original plot the *New Arcadia* has something of an episodic quality. It reads rather like a story-collection, comprised of heroic battle-scenes, political plots, tragic love-stories and nugatory offerings like those of Miso and Mopsa (*NA* 307–12). Little is known of how Sidney went about revising his text, but the episodic structure appears to have given him the flexibility to continually add stories to his initial narrative, just as one could add new sonnets into an existing sequence without destroying its underlying logic. Subsequent writers looking to the *New Arcadia* for source material took advantage of several notable narrative chunks that could function autonomously from the overall story in their own work. Shakespeare famously used the story of the Paphlagonian king and his sons Leonatus and Plexirtus (*NA* 275–82) for the Gloucester subplot of *King Lear*. Similarly, the tragic tale of Argalus and Parthenia is reworked by Francis Quarles (1629) and Henry Glapthorne (1639) in poetry and drama respectively.

Binding this fragmentary structure together is a series of chains of cause and effect: of lovers to be pursued; quests to be fulfilled; revenges to be exacted; disguises to be revealed;

prophesies to be understood. Indeed the *New Arcadia* exemplifies the teleological yet dilatory characteristics of the romance genre identified by Patricia Parker, of how romance 'simultaneously quests for and postpones a particular end, objective, or object'.[3] Even more so than in the earlier version, Sidney invites speculation and interpretation of characters and objects in the narrative through onomastic and heraldic clues and frequent episodes centred on veiling and recognition. Pyrocles, for example, hopes to gain news of Amphialus through donning pieces of his armour and learning 'by them that should know that armour' (*NA* 119). He is soon 'misread' by Helen, though learns much about Amphialus. As is common in chivalric romance, armour serves as an expedient screen, allowing characters to meet and clash yet defer discovery of identity. Along with the participants in Phalantus's tournament, we are left to wonder momentarily as to the identity of the 'ill-appointed' knight (Pyrocles) who defeats the equally enigmatic Black Knight (Musidorus) (*NA* 165–8). Deferred revelations can also have tragic consequences, as in the story of Tydeus and Telenor whom Plexirtus tricks into fighting a fatal combat with each other (*NA* 361–3).

The copiousness of the plot is certainly matched by the richness of Sidney's language, and the text has long been admired for its style and rhetoric as much as for its content. Sidney is praised by John Hoskins in his *Directions for Speech and Style* (1599) as a master of rhetorical elaboration or *periphrasis*. He cites examples, such as when

> [i]nstead of 'Plangus' speech began to be suspected', it is said: 'Plangus' speech began to be translated into the language of suspicion'. And this of purpose did he write, to keep his style from baseness: as, being to name 'a thresher', he called him 'one of Ceres' servants'.[4]

Exuberant linguistic play can also be seen in Sidney's frequent use of conceits, as in the often-cited example of Pamela sewing (*NA* 483), the magnetism of Pyrocles–Zelmane's soul to Philoclea through his/her body (*NA* 235), or the description of Miso and Mopsa helping the princesses disrobe, who 'like a couple of foreswat [sweating] melters, were getting the pure silver of their bodies out of the ure [ore] of their garments' (*NA* 285). In each case there is a sensuousness in the elaborate detail, as if enjoyment of language were a surrogate for physical stimulation. If Sidney's imagery inclines towards the hyperbolic it is not without good reason. The following description of Philoclea's torture enacts a verbal assault upon the captive princess just as violent as the physical torments she endures at Cecropia's hand:

> at length abominable rage carried her to absolute tyrannies; so that taking with her certain old women (of wicked dispositions, and apt for envy's sake to be cruel to youth and beauty) with a countenance empoisoned with malice, flew to the sweet Philoclea, as if so many kites should come about a white dove; and matching violent gestures with mischievous threatenings, she having a rod in her hand (like a fury that should carry wood to the burning of Diana's temple) fell to scourge that most beautiful body; love in vain holding the shield of beauty against her blind cruelty. The sun drew clouds up to hide his face from so pitiful a sight, and the very stone walls did yield drops of sweat for agony of such a mischief: each senseless thing had sense of pity; only they that had sense were senseless. (*NA* 551–2)

The characters' own rhetorical skills, demonstrated through orations and debates, remain at the heart of the narrative. Set-pieces such as the princes' debate on love and Philanax's plea to Basilius (now presented as a letter) are complemented by Pyrocles's placatory oration to the Helots (*NA* 100–103) and Pamela's magnificent refutation of Cecropia's argument that it is fear and ignorance that engender religious belief, a defining moment for Sidney's heroine (*NA* 483–92).

From the opening of the *New Arcadia* and mournful complaints of Klaius and Strephon there is an evident shift to a far more serious tone, engendered to some degree by the greater emphasis on human limitations and political realism noted above. There are many examples of chivalric ideals seen in the princes' repeated acts of self-sacrifice and in the conduct afforded to wounded (noble) enemies, as when Pyrocles proposes to the injured Amphialus 'though I love not your person ... I pray you, let us take care of your wound, upon condition you shall hereafter promise that a more knightly combat shall be performed between us' (*NA* 294). But the text shows a great number of such wounds (and wounded characters) and presents Arcadia and its surrounding lands in a particularly violent light. Musidorus enters Arcadia via the 'civil wildness' of war-torn Laconia and soon persuades Kalander to mount a rescue attempt for Clitophon that pitches Arcadians and Helots into a vicious battle. Martial sports at Phalantus's and Helen's tournaments, for which Sidney provides extensive technical details of armour, swordplay and tactics, are eclipsed by the violent manner in which the princes punish the rebels in book 2 for deigning to raise themselves from quotidian occupations like butchery or milling to the ranks of fighting men. A particularly cruel fate awaits the 'poor painter' who watches the combats to learn how to better depict a violent scene, but has his hands struck off by Musidorus (*NA* 380–81). 'And so', concludes Sidney with bitter irony, 'the painter returned well skilled in wounds, but with never a hand to perform his skill'. What are we to make of such a gratuitous scene? Some critics see Sidney verbally punishing those who choose to represent rebellion. For others the painter has committed an aesthetic crime in desiring merely to copy slavishly from existing natural forms rather than create things anew (as Sidney advocates in the *Defence*) and fashion forms 'such as never were in nature' (*MW* 216). Further horrors of war are shown in book 3 in the successive, largely futile battles against Amphialus that eventually cost the lives of Argalus and Parthenia. Sidney continues to interrogate the commonplaces of romance through juxtaposition of chivalric ideals with the far darker, more visceral implications of combat and soldiery.

Sidney is equally concerned to recalibrate how one perceives the nature of amorous elements in his romance and plays up the princes' heroic actions at the same time as removing some of the more morally dubious incidents found in the original version. In particular, in the final two books of the 1593 edition emended by Mary Sidney in accordance with her brother's intentions, Musidorus's abortive rape of Pamela and Pyrocles's copulation with Philoclea are removed. The wording of the prophecy and trial indictment are also altered to emphasize the political, rather than moral, nature of the princes' perceived crime. Rape is later redeployed to heighten Cecropia's villainy as she counsels Amphialus to take the captive Philoclea by force (*NA* 532–4). Points of erotic titillation remain, however, as when Pyrocles witnesses Philoclea bathing naked and goes on to sing – now with some basis in empirical observation – the reassigned blazon

'What tongue can her perfections tell'.

One of the results of Sidney's attempts to make the princes less morally ambiguous is that many of the questions previously raised by their actions about love, politics and chivalric conduct are now revisited in examining the actions and motivations of Amphialus, perhaps the most intriguing character in the *New Arcadia*. Amphialus's presentation is a good example of the emphasis Sidney now places on constructing central characters with a much greater sense of complexity and interiority. Although taken from Homer's *Odyssey*, even Amphialus's name – derived from Greek *ampho*, meaning 'both' or 'two-sided' – reflects the ambivalence of his character. As noted above, Amphialus's loyalties are questioned from the outset, but when we learn more about him from Helen, his virtuous nurturing by Timotheus appears to have effaced any trace of an affinity with his wicked mother Cecropia. He was commonly known as 'courteous Amphialus' and together with companion Philoxenus occupied himself with adventures comparable to those of Musidorus's and Pyrocles's youth (*NA* 123). He is repeatedly shown to be an excellent, honourable warrior and a cunning politician. Yet Amphialus is also guilty of replicating Basilius's errors and pursuing personal, amorous motives above all other concerns. His desire for Philoclea not only initiates the war in book 3 but perpetuates the bloodshed:

> But no sword paid so large a tribute of souls to the eternal kingdom as that of Amphialus; who like a tiger from whom a company of wolves did seek to ravish a new gotten prey, so he (remembering they came to take away Philoclea) did labour to make valour, strength, choler and hatred to answer the proportion of his love which was infinite. (*NA* 469)

Sidney uses Amphialus to stretch to its limits the paradox of the lover-knight – something central to chivalric romance – and he is the focus of two incidents in which the language and logic of chivalry are interrogated and found wanting. The first is when Amphialus attempts to play the Petrarchan love-servant with the imprisoned Philoclea and is reminded that declarations of his being wounded or constrained by love are emptily rhetorical compared to the physical constraints placed upon the princesses (*NA* 449–51). The second follows Amphialus's defeat of

Parthenia, when he temporarily rejects chivalric trappings and breaks his sword (*NA* 531). He earlier abandoned his armour after being forced to kill Philoxenus (*NA* 127). Amphialus's ultimate tragedy is that he never really rejects arms for long and is led to confront further martial challenges by his misguided devotion to the unyielding Philoclea, bearing new armour that reflects his intractable position and carrying the princess's knives, 'the only token of her forced favour' (*NA* 535).

Sidney also creates a much greater sense of psychological complexity for the female characters of the *New Arcadia*, working through each nuance of Philoclea's realization of her love for Pyrocles–Zelmane, for example, and expanding upon his earlier presentation of how love and jealousy torment Gynecia (*NA* 237–44, 376–8). In both cases Sidney attempts to suggest a credible set of human responses to events and anatomizes the motives and implications of his characters' actions, again with the intention of providing models for his readers' emulation. The depth of interiority suggested for the princesses really comes into play in book 3 as Cecropia mentally tortures her prisoners. Pamela in particular stands out as a model of constancy and reason, more than adequately equipped with a mental integrity enabling her to face down Cecropia in successive verbal encounters that challenge and ultimately affirm Pamela's personal and spiritual qualities. Thereafter Cecropia can only resort to grisly, non-verbal spectacles to try and trick the princesses and Pyrocles–Zelmane into submission. Though Basilius and Musidorus use physical force against Cecropia's extra-mural armies, the real victories are achieved within the castle walls through the princesses' inward strengths. Throughout the *New Arcadia* Sidney continues to cross-examine the nature of female virtue through presenting a succession of active, strong-willed female characters, including the princesses, Gynecia, Parthenia, Cecropia, Dido, Helen, Erona, Andromana and Artaxia. Zelmane must also be added to this list, not least for 'her' reminder to the rebels that 'a woman may well speak to such men who have forgotten all man-like government' (*NA* 384). Some of these are clearly models for imitation, some are exemplars of vice to be avoided, and others (such as Helen and Erona) are harder to judge, forcing us away from the character types found in the *Old Arcadia* and towards a mode that attempts to demonstrate and question nuances of motive and personality.

One can still trace elements of personal allegory in the *New Arcadia* though these are greatly downplayed. The most notable example is the reduced presence of Philisides who now only appears as a pastoral knight at the Iberian jousts in a combat with Lelius (possibly representing Sir Henry Lee). Philisides no longer sings his love songs to Mira, many of which are reassigned to other characters, though there remains a subtle authorial allusion to Sidney's Stella in his renamed mistress, 'the Star whereby his course was only directed' (*NA* 353). Philisides's diminished role parallels the impersonalization of the narratorial voice in the *New Arcadia* and further signals Sidney's manipulation of genre as he adopts a presentational mode more commonly identified with epic. In his bridging passage between the revised and original material written for the 1621 *Arcadia*, Sir William Alexander nevertheless maintains an explicit connection between Philisides and Sidney, paying tribute to the latter through his poignant description of the former's death (*NA* 614, 864). Elsewhere echoes of Sidney's parents have been identified in Argalus and Parthenia – the latter's facial disfiguration by Demagoras reflecting Lady Mary's smallpox scars, and the description of Kalander's house seen as a glowing representation of the family seat at Penshurst. Historicist readings of the villainous Cecropia have proved equally hard to resist, though critics are divided as to whether she represents Mary, Queen of Scots, Catherine de' Medici, or, in similar fashion to Spenser's Duessa, the Catholic Church as a whole. It is also difficult not to identify avatars of Elizabeth in several of the new regal characters, though interpretative ambiguity still pervades. Helen's tournaments evoke Elizabeth's tilts, but how does one view her relationship with Amphialus that has led her from her land and duties? Andromana – aged and with 'exceeding red hair' – bears the greatest physical likeness to Sidney's sovereign though her unsuccessful wooing of the princes and eventual suicide forestalls an unproblematic identification. More than anything, the *New Arcadia*'s multiple queens show Sidney grappling with the central dilemma of representing queenship under Elizabeth: does one present the queen within a text as she actually is, or project an idealized image of how she *should* be?

Despite the emphasis on positivist, political motives for events in Arcadia, the revised text shows how Sidney continues to experiment with notions of Protestant poetics. In particular he confronts the seemingly contradictory situation where his choice of form, heroic romance, predicates a narrative centred on active martial works which is at odds with a Calvinist world-view and its attendant ideas of human incapacity. Sidney addresses this quandary by stressing the limitations of heroic action alone, which merely threatens to perpetuate endless violence, and by demonstrating his heroes' inadequacy and continued subjugation to higher forces beyond their control. Amphialus is a particular case in point: his final speech details a litany of wrong choices, mistakenly killed friends, and bungled plans, including his attempt at suicide (*NA* 573–4). At the same time Sidney repeatedly shows that the most significant 'saving' agent in the text, the means by which characters gain redress for human fallibility, is providence. The idea of a divine order underlying the seemingly chaotic web of natural acts and causes in the *New Arcadia* is of immense importance for Sidney's reconfiguration of his chosen form. There are no real instances of magic in this romance, instead (suggests Evans) the benevolent supernatural force of providence works to fulfil the prophecy's terms (*NA* 34). Pamela's prayer during her captivity is the definitive statement of belief in a controlling divine order, made all the more powerful through its utterance by a supposedly pagan figure (*NA* 463–4). Charles I copied and used the prayer for his own solace whilst imprisoned, as he sets out in *Eikon Basilike*, though he was criticized for doing so in Milton's reactionary *Eikonoklastes* (1649). Throughout the *New Arcadia* characters are continually divided and then reunited seemingly by chance (as in Musidorus and Pyrocles's encounter during the Laconian civil war), or they are saved by the intervention of an external, occasionally misattributed, power (as when Euarchus happens to enter Arcadia in the revised book 5 to unite divisions – so says Philanax – at heaven's behest (*NA* 785)). The most threatening force within the revised books, Cecropia, is brought down through her own accidental fall from a roof, rather than through one of the princes' actions. Sidney thus confronts potential critics who might condemn romance as unproductive 'books of fayned cheualrie' through stressing that the greatest heroism is demonstrated by those characters showing patience, inner strength and resolution in adversity. One might have expected Sidney to utilize heroic romance as an opportunity to unambiguously project his frustrated martial ambitions. But his interests appear to lie far more in what he could achieve through writing, in particular how he could adapt the heroic poem for purposes consonant with Protestant didacticism.

The revised book 3 breaks off mid-sentence during a fight between Pyrocles and Anaxius as Sidney abandoned the text, perhaps temporarily, either to prepare for an embassy to France in July 1584 or to write his *Defence of Leicester* in response to the libellous pamphlet *Leicester's Commonwealth* printed that year. Sidney's defence was never published, but it combined a concerted attempt to stress his Dudley connection with scathing criticism of Catholic exiles and supporters. There are several other works that Sidney started around this time though never finished. One such project was his translation of the Psalms. Vernacular translations of the Psalms were an important part of Reformation culture as they combined a strictly scriptural text with a more communal, congregational formal mode. There were many versified versions produced during the sixteenth century, the most popular being that by Thomas Sternhold and John Hopkins (published 1562). Metrical psalters were also ideologically associated with English and continental militant Protestantism. Sidney's closest model for the forty-three translated psalms was the French psalter by Clément Marot and Théodore de Bèze (1562). Like Marot, Sidney deployed a huge variety of metrical and rhyming forms, using a different scheme for each psalm, and his translations were a markedly new technical development compared to the plodding metres of 'Sternhold-Hopkins'. For this reason, some critics place the collection alongside Sidney's earlier experiments with English versification, though critical consensus now dates the psalms to the mid-1580s, treating them as a virtuoso display of metrical accomplishment and a further attempt to integrate English poetry with a commitment to Protestant cultural forms. Sidney's sister completed the collection after his death, as discussed in the next chapter. Sidney writes in the *Defence* that the metrical 'rules' for the Psalms are yet to be found (*MW* 215), though the paraphrase collection can perhaps be viewed as the Sidneys' creative attempt to supply their own native version in the interim.

Sidney also began to translate a treatise defending Christianity against atheism, Mornay's *De la vérité de la religion chrestienne*, which was professedly completed by Arthur Golding and published as *The Trewnesse of the Christian Religion* (1587), though the extant text is now thought to be wholly Golding's. Several contemporary sources refer to Sidney's now-lost translation of du Bartas's poem on the first week of Creation, *La semaine*, probably produced post-1582. Although all of these works are incomplete, taken together with the revised *Arcadia*, the picture that emerges of Sidney's later writing demonstrates a consistent interest in refashioning a devoutly Protestant English literature that is influenced though not circumscribed by continental models.

In July 1585 Sidney was made Master of Ordnance, though in the same November he received the kind of employment he had long sought. To check increasing Spanish aggression in the Netherlands Elizabeth sanctioned military intervention, headed by Leicester, to aid the Dutch. As part of the expeditionary force Sidney was made Governor of Flushing (Vlissingen). For eleven months he struggled with poorly paid and ill-equipped troops to mount limited military campaigns against the Spanish until, on 22 September 1586, he was wounded in the thigh by a musket-ball during a skirmish near the town of Zutphen. Posthumous myths surrounding Sidney's heroic fall attribute his wound to a chivalrous decision not to wear leg-armour (or *cuisses*) because a fellow soldier lacked such protection. Greville, who remained in England during the Dutch expedition, also records the famous story of Sidney offering his water-bottle to a more wounded common soldier, claiming 'Thy necessity is yet greater than mine' (Gouws, 77), though this appears to echo an incident in Plutarch's life of Alexander the Great more than it reflects real events at Zutphen (*MW* 408). Whilst he lay wounded Sidney is said to have written a (now-lost) poem on his injury 'La Cuisse Rompue' which was set to music and sung to him, and a later reference by Edward, Lord Herbert of Cherbury, claims that Sidney continued to write until the very end.[5] After bequeathing his books to Greville and Dyer and his sword to Robert Devereux, second Earl of Essex, Sidney died of gangrene at Arnhem on 17 October 1586. His body was returned to England and on 16 February 1587 he was buried at St Paul's Cathedral following a huge funeral procession, on a scale only matched in more modern times by those for Winston Churchill or Diana, Princess of Wales. It was attended by hundreds of noblemen, gentlemen and soldiers (though not by the queen) and reproduced the same year in a magnificent series of engravings published by Thomas Lant. Sidney's death prompted an outpouring of literary responses, including elegy collections from Oxford, Cambridge and Leiden universities, and separate memorial offerings ranging from Churchyard's brief *Epitaph of Sir Philip Sidney* (1587) through to Spenser's 1595 *Colin Clouts Come Home Againe* volume, which included elegies by Raleigh and Bryskett. The volume also featured 'The Dolefull Lay of Clorinda', which although sometimes ascribed to Mary Sidney (Clorinda being the Sidney-figure Astrophil's sister) was probably written by Spenser appropriating Mary's voice and standpoint. A contemporary diarist epitomized the common sense of loss to English cultural life and politics felt at Sidney's passing in claiming that 'the very hope of our age seemeth to be utterly extinguished in him'.[6]

It is from this point onwards that the mythologization and 'use' of Sidney really develops and it has been suggested that even the pomp of his funeral served to distract public attention away from the execution of Mary, Queen of Scots, carried out eight days before. A series of early biographies repeatedly refashion different versions of Sidney for a variety of ends. Seasoned elegist George Whetstone was moved by other enterprising writers' hasty attempts to cash in on Sidney's memory and sought to offer his own verse biography for those that loved him 'or would be like vnto him'.[7] He dwells upon his subject's literary accomplishments, praising the *Arcadia* though also misattributing Spenser's *Shepheardes Calender* to him, clearly signalling Sidney's close identification with the pastoral genre. Thomas Moffet, both physician and neighbour to the Wilton household, wrote his *Nobilis* (*c*.1592–3) with the specific intention of offering models of virtuous conduct for Sidney's nephew William Herbert. Moffet repeatedly dismisses the majority of Sidney's writings as trivial juvenalia, implausibly dating the *Arcadia* and *Astrophil* to his pre-Oxford days and foregrounding his active, public profile. He approved, however, of the Psalms and du Bartas translations. Sidney's life and death were also considered worthy enough objects of public and national significance for inclusion in Holinshed's 1587 *Chronicles* and John Stow's *Annales* (1592). The most extensive mythologizing account is Greville's *Life of Sidney* (written c.1610–14), originally intended as an introduction to a collection of Greville's own works. Refused access to the required source documents for an official history of Elizabeth's reign by James I's chief minister Robert Cecil, Greville composed the *Life* as an extended *occupatio*, signalling throughout that Sidney's biography provides the opportunity to advance an idealized history of Elizabeth's reign and policies. Greville draws contrasts between 'those active times and the narrow salves of this effeminate age' to obliquely criticize James's rule (Gouws, 7). He stresses Sidney's active engagement with international politics, though downplays his antagonistic relationship with Elizabeth.

Just as the line blurs between man and myth, so the boundary between Sidney's works and their continuations, re-presentations and imitations soon becomes far less distinct. Although reporting that Sidney on his deathbed apparently ordered that the *Arcadia* manuscripts be burnt (just as Virgil ultimately condemned his *Aeneid*), in 1590 Greville published an edition of the revised portions (only), in part to pre-empt publication of a feared pirated edition of the *Old Arcadia*. Writing to Walsingham in 1586 Greville exhibits a concern to ensure that Sidney's reputation was founded on the more religious writings produced in his final years. To highlight an explicitly moral reading of the *New Arcadia* Greville (possibly aided by Matthew Gwinne and John Florio) provided his own headnotes to each of his chapter divisions, signalling the exempla to be identified at each point and framing the book as a work of Neostoic moral and political philosophy. This is also the way that the revised *Arcadia* is employed in Greville's *Life* and in John Hayward's history of Elizabeth's reign (composed 1612).[8] Sidney's sister, however, sought to fashion a rather different image of her brother and published an edition of *Arcadia* in 1593 including both the reworked books 1 to 3 and the original matter from books 3 to 5, though the latter material was also revised (as mentioned above) both to remove the princes' sexual exploits and to preserve consistency of names and references across all five books. The preface to the 1593 edition by the Pembrokes' secretary Hugh Sanford clearly casts the composite *Arcadia* as the more authoritative version: 'The disfigured face, gentle reader, wherewith this work not long since appeared to the common view, moved that noble lady to whose honour consecrated, to whose protection it was committed, to take in hand the wiping away those spots wherewith the beauties thereof were unworthily blemished' (*NA* 59). The 1593 edition sees Mary beginning to fashion her brother far more as an authoritative literary figure whose writings are not simply idle toys but a worthy means of perpetuating his fame and memory. As Joel Davis argues, the 1593 *Arcadia* provided the foundation for a continued identification based on literary tradition (particularly relating to pastoral poetry) between the countess and her Sidney heritage, as the literary equivalent of the Sidney family estate.[9] Sanford's preface closed by promising further editorial labours and in 1598 Mary published a folio collection of all of Sidney's main works under the heading *The Countesse of Pembroke's Arcadia*. Again the volume explicitly signals a close identification between Sidney's writings, pastoral poetry and Mary's involvement. The 1598 volume established a credible precedent for publishing editions of authors' collected works that undoubtedly influenced subsequent folio collections, such as those of Spenser (1611), Jonson (1616) and Shakespeare (1623). The published *Arcadia* prompted a number of continuations and translations during the early seventeenth century and also provided plentiful material for the popular stage as, for example, in the anonymous *Mucedorus* (1598), John Day's *Ile of Gulls* (1606) and James Shirley's *Arcadia* (1640).

Detailing Sidney's critical heritage in full would require a book at least as long as the *New Arcadia*. But what becomes clear from very early on, indeed from within his own lifetime, is that Sidney's status as an authoritative literary practitioner and innovator was widely acknowledged, and he would serve as a model for authorship, both at court and (posthumously) in print, that influenced Spenser, Jonson, and the immediate Sidney family, amongst many others. It is this version of Sidney, rather than the pious statesman fashioned by Greville, that long formed the greater part of his posthumous reputation. However, as the previous chapters have shown, the struggle to integrate (or at least explore the relationship between) seemingly opposed traditions and structures remained a productive, animating force within Sidney's writings, and perhaps he himself would not have recognized as much of an irreconcilable difference between the particular constructions of his life and works advanced by his sister and best friend.

6

The Sidney Circle

MARY SIDNEY

As we have already seen, Mary Sidney played a vital role in both preparing authorized versions of her brother's major works and shaping his posthumous reputation as a literary and cultural authority. Critics have also increasingly focused their attention not only on Mary's own writings but on how she fashions a literary reputation for herself. The notion of female authorship in early modern England was immensely problematic and challenged the traditional formulation, drawn from contemporary models of female conduct, that women should be chaste, silent and obedient. Unrestrained female speech, and by implication unchecked expression in writing and print, was particularly associated with sexual forwardness and impropriety. Despite their more progressive stance towards the female intellect, sixteenth-century humanists such as Juan Luis Vives and Sir Thomas More, together with numerous contemporary Reformist authorities, had written extensively on the virtues of female silence and passivity, and had established that a woman's sole preserve was the domestic sphere. Silence coupled with obedience to one's husband within the household was supported by St Paul's frequently evoked exhortation against women speaking in church in 1 Corinthians 14:34–5. This was amplified in the authorized 'Homily on the state of Matrimony' in the second Anglican *Book of Homilies* (1562–3). With the exception of works on devotional subjects, original compositions by women were constrained by the prevailing injunctions against female speech and the attendant view that any such writing lacked legitimacy. The concept of female authorship itself was thus inherently undermined by the questionable status of female authority as a whole.

But the world of letters was not as exclusively male as such a social milieu might suggest, and a number of different 'auxiliary' literary roles have been identified through which early modern women began both to wield a certain amount of control and influence and to develop further strategies of legitimation. Patronage was one way in which royal and aristocratic women might have their names put to a work, usually through dedications and addresses, and exercise a level of benevolent power to make a work possible through providing material reward or employment. Translation also provided a means of establishing a legitimate form of writing project for women writers, for through the rewriting of an existing text the translator inherently implies an inferiority to, or at very least a lesser degree of agency than the (male) author of the original. Mary Sidney was both a celebrated patron and a skilled translator, but she also stressed her close association with her brother and his writings as a key authorizing gesture when constructing her own literary reputation. Following her marriage to the Earl of Pembroke in 1577 Mary continued to identify herself as a Sidney through retaining the family coat of arms. After 1586, as her late brother's literary executor, Mary worked hard to consolidate, defend and extend the Sidney family's literary legacy by committing her brother's work to print during the 1590s, thereby widening his potential audience, and by fashioning a role for herself through which she might continue to embody her brother's ideals for poetry, politics and religion. The Sidney identity was therefore something that Mary both nurtured in her brother's name and drew upon for herself.

One of the ways that she does this is through acting as patron to a number of those writers who had known Sidney and shared his experiments with English versification, and fostering a loosely constituted coterie of writers connected with her household at Wilton that included Daniel, Fraunce, Moffet and the prolific poet Nicholas Breton. One should be cautious not to construct too expansive a conception of the Sidney circle's membership and organization. It would be wrong to imply that Wilton was continuously peopled with Elizabethan literary luminaries or that every one of the many would-be clients dedicating their work to Mary was known to or supported by her, as earlier critics keen to discover extensive patronage networks have a tendency to suggest. But for twenty-five years following Sidney's death Mary continues to make Wilton what Breton (writing in 1597) calls 'a kinde of little Court' comparable to the rarefied community of Urbino portrayed by Castiglione. Breton continues by describing Wilton as a place of honour, virtue, reward and pious study. Sidney had of course already made Wilton his home whilst writing the *Old Arcadia,* and celebrated the locality of his sister's household in his poem 'The Seven Wonders of England'. The combination of courtliness and piety that Breton identifies is emblematic of the complex interplay of seemingly opposing values encountered throughout Sidney's writings and it is clear that Mary, through her own works, was continuing to explore the relationship between the secular and sacred, and between worldly instability and eternal constancy.

Mary had shared in the production and reception of most if not all of Sidney's works, though she probably only began writing herself following her brother's death. The majority of her extant writings are translations and draw upon her thorough tutoring – very likely alongside her brothers – in the French, Italian, Latin, Greek and Hebrew languages. As mentioned above, translation was considered an entirely appropriate kind of literary activity for women, but it also offered Mary a means to work with existing forms and narratives to foreground female experiences and perspectives. Two of her translations address death and mourning, a somewhat understandable subject given that she also lost both her parents in the same year that her brother died. In 1590 she translated *A Discourse of Life and Death* by Sidney's friend Philippe de Mornay, a treatise that reflects on the frustrations and miseries encountered at each stage of earthly life and scorns the vanity of worldly riches. At the core of the treatise is the Stoic idea that detachment from worldly desires provides the means to endure misfortune and death. Such extended advocacy of a model of patient, inner endurance, rather than heroic action, provided Mary with not simply personal consolation but a formulation of heroism that would prove particularly apposite for representing the demise of female characters in several of her other translations. It also recalls Pamela's reasoned response to adversity during the captivity episode of the *New Arcadia*.

Mornay's treatise dealt more with misfortunes afflicting the male sphere of active public life, notwithstanding the fact that it could be readily *applied* to female experiences. However, in her translation of Petrarch's *Triumph of Death* Mary could activate a language of idealized love and spiritual resolve that focused upon the final interaction between Petrarch's poet-figure and his beloved Laura. Written during the 1340–50s, Petrarch's *Trionfi* were a series of dream visions presenting the triumphs of Love, Chastity, Death, Fame, Time and Eternity, with each concept overthrowing that which precedes it. They were immensely popular and hugely influential throughout the medieval and Renaissance periods. *The Triumph of Death* sees the figure of Death coming to take the young, chaste Laura to join the 'never-numbered summe' of the dead. It dwells first upon Laura's acquiescence and the peaceful departure of her spirit and then on Petrarch's subsequent vision of Laura in which she consoles him about the nature of death and instructs him on how to live, now she has gone. Mary's version of the poem is remarkable on purely formal grounds and notable for the accuracy and fluency of its translation, preserving as it does for the first time in English Petrarch's *terza rima* stanzas. What really stands out though is Mary's presentation of Laura and the impassioned language through which the heroine counsels the poet to abandon the 'flames' of worldly desire that torment him, continuing to evoke incendiary imagery used in Petrarch's amatory lyrics and their numerous imitations, and assuring him that she had felt similar inward desires throughout his suit, though controlled her response through exercising reason and privileging their joint sense of honour. Sidney's Astrophil was offered a similar form of idealized love in Sonnet 62, though his desire for physical fulfilment ultimately gets the better of him. The poignant final moments of Petrarch's vision see the poet imploring Laura:

> Ladie (quoth I) yor words most sweetelie kinde
> Have easie made, what ever erst I bare,
> But what is left of yow to live behinde.
> Therefore to knowe this, my onelie care,
> If sloe or swift shall com or meeting-daye.
> Shee parting saide, As my conjectures are,
> Thow without me long time on earth shalt staie.
>
> (Hannay, vol. 1, 282)

It is also tempting to read these concluding lines – as many have – as Mary's own farewell to her brother. Again, the text chosen for translation foregrounds how inward mastery of one's feelings towards death and love may be construed as a form of heroism. But this time such qualities are directly authorized by a female protagonist to the point that, as Mary Ellen Lamb writes, 'Through Laura women could perceive themselves as spiritual authorities, bearing upon their virtuous shoulders the responsibilities for their husbands' immortal souls'.[1] Such an authoritative female model was never shared with a wider audience and only exists in a sole manuscript, a letter sent by Harington to Lucy Russell, Countess of Bedford in 1600.

The translation of Mornay's treatise was far more widely known. It was published in 1592 together with another text that explores female responses to adversity, Mary's translation of Robert Garnier's French closet drama *Marc Antoine* (originally published in 1578). Garnier's play was of the Neostoic Senecan tradition popular in contemporary France. Designed primarily for private reading rather than public performance, closet drama is noticeably different from the plays written for the early modern popular stage with which most modern readers will be more familiar. The play (translated into English as *Antonius*) adheres relatively closely to the neoclassical unities of place, time and action and lays great emphasis on formal speeches and debates, alternating between characters' extensive philosophical musings on fate and personal responsibility and taut stichomythic exchanges. As in classical tragedy, protracted verbal interaction takes the place of any representation of significant action and key events such as Antonie's suicide attempt and removal to Cleopatra's tomb are reported rather than shown. *Antonius* is set following the defeat of Antonie and Cleopatra's forces at the battle of Actium and presents a series of loosely connected scenes showing the varying responses of the doomed lovers as they face the impending conquest of Octavius. Antonie increasingly blames his misfortune upon his destructive desire to enjoy the worldly pleasure represented by Cleopatra and his consequent derogation of his duties as a soldier and leader. To redeem himself he vows to make an honourable end by taking his life. The art of dying well is a major theme here, as it is in the other translations, and finds its best articulation in Cleopatra.

Although aware that the lovers' downfall is the result of their unchecked passion, Mary's Cleopatra is presented not as the seductive temptress found in Shakespeare's play but as a noble, Stoic figure concerned for her people, children and husband. Her dying speech includes a request to be buried wrapped in the same winding-sheet as Antonie, though never fully rejects her physical passions as she smothers his body in kisses in the closing lines. *Antonius* offers a further exploration of the fatal consequences for rulers who place private desires above public responsibilities. Garnier himself wrote against the backdrop of the French wars of religion and all three of his Roman plays reflect on the horrors of civil discord. Mary's choice of text allows her the opportunity to adopt the voice of a passionate worldly woman but also enables a ventriloquized promotion of a form of female heroism based on constancy and dignity when faced with adversity. Tragedy is generated in *Antonius* through accenting Cleopatra's realization of how these latter ideal qualities are irrevocably compromised by worldly desires. We are again involved with a key source of tension found within *Astrophil* and the *Arcadias*.

Mary was certainly following in her brother's stead through choosing to translate Garnier's closet drama, as it comes close to the neoclassical dramatic model of 'stately speeches', off-stage report and conformity to unities favoured in the *Defence*. *Antonius* initiated a short-lived vogue for closet drama amongst those connected with the Sidney circle: Thomas Kyd translated Garnier's *Cornélie* (1594); Daniel wrote *Cleopatra* (1594) and *Philotas* (1595), the former a continuation of Mary's play; and Greville composed his *Mustapha* and *Alaham* during the same period. Despite the Sidney seal of approval neoclassical drama was never successfully developed on the English popular stage. However, Mary's translation should be recognized and acclaimed for its contribution to the tradition of historical drama that would flourish in theatres during the 1590s, for its attempts to render Neo-Senecan drama into blank verse (rather than Garnier's alexandrines), and for developing the practice of commenting on contemporary native affairs using dramatized Roman history. Shakespeare's *Antony and Cleopatra* reveals that he certainly knew *Antonius* and drew on Mary's sympathetic portrayal of Cleopatra when depicting the heroine's enduring passion for Antony in the play's final scene.

The finest and most celebrated of Mary's works are her metrical paraphrases of the Psalms, a project of her brother's that she continues after his death and that she would revise for over a decade. According to Daniel's dedication to *Cleopatra*, it was the metrical psalms that would outlive Mary and the Wilton household, providing her with a form of textual immortality and eternal fame. The psalms offer the best example of how Mary could actively continue to work 'with' her brother through first imitating and then surpassing his poetry, gaining cultural and social authority both from working within Sidney's literary tradition and by appropriating the words of the original psalmist King David via those of the contemporary translators (including Marot and Bèze) that she uses as her source text. A masterpiece of creative syncretism, the psalm paraphrases are a far less conservative translation than Mary's other works. Sidney translated only forty-three of the Psalms, leaving Mary to complete the remaining 102, which included the twenty-two poems of Psalm 119. She also modified seven of Sidney's psalms. Whilst conforming to the notion that translation of pious texts was somehow less creative and thus less transgressive than original composition, the stunning variety of 126 metres and verse forms that Mary uses provides as much, if not more, of a display of poetic prowess as her brother's paraphrases. The title page to one of the psalms manuscripts explicitly makes the point that these were not only 'Begun by the Noble and Learned gentleman Sir Phillip Sidney knight' but that they are consciously conceived as a literary achievement: 'translated into divers and sundry kindes of verse, more Rare and Excellent for the Method and Varietie then ever yet hath been done in English' (Hannay, vol. 2, 314). Mary's psalms incorporate use of the sestina (Psalm 49), rhyme royal (Psalms 51, 63), *ottava rima* (Psalm 78), *terza rima* (Psalm 119 H), the Spenserian stanza (Psalm 100), an acrostic spelling 'Prais[e] the lord' (Psalm 117), together with nearly a dozen exercises in quantitative verse. They also contain several verbal allusions to Sidney's poetry. For example, Psalm 73 begins with the speaker struggling to comprehend the seeming contradiction of how the 'wicked' prevail despite God's authority:

> It is most true that god to Israell,
> I meane to men of undefiled hartes,
> is only good, and nought but good impartes.
>
> (Hannay, vol. 2, Psalm 73, ll. 1–3)

Sidney uses an identical phrasing ('It is most true') in Sonnet 5 of *Astrophil* to question why, despite his realization that true beauty is an 'inward light', he should be drawn to Stella by purely physical desire.

Just as Sidney's sonnet sequence utilized a vocabulary of frustration and submission to a higher authority found in both the Petrarchan and Protestant traditions, so the Psalms offered Mary a means to articulate the same sense of passion, frustration, anxiety and consequent self-examination expressed throughout *Astrophil*. She could become, in Beth Wynne Fisken's words, 'an active participant in her verse-translations of the Psalms in a way that would have been impossible for her within the conventions of the sonnet form, where even a women speaker imagined by a woman writer is limited to passive suffering and endurance'.[2] There is a directness and urgency in Mary's psalms, largely absent in those of Sidney, which is particularly evident in many of the opening addresses and invocations, as in Psalm 119 E ('Explaine, ô lord, the way to me,/ that thy divine edicts enfold') or Psalm 121 ('What? and doe I behold the lovely mountaines,/ Whence comes all my reliefe, my aid, my comfort?'). Again we might look to *Astrophil* for better comparisons as Mary enacts a parody of the language, emotions and situations found in love poetry; see for example the sensuous Psalm 63:

> And lo, ev'n heer I mind thee in my bedd,
> and interupt my sleepes with nightly thought,
> how thou hast bene the target of my hedd,
> how thy wings shadow hath my safty wrought.
> and though my body from thy view be brought;
> yet fixt on thee my loving soule remaines,
> whose right hand from falling, me retaines.
>
> (Hannay, vol. 2, Psalm 63, ll. 15–21)

The array of voices adopted by the psalmist, ranging from the admonitory down to the penitent, further furnished Mary with the opportunity to play a variety of roles incorporating both the virtuous (Psalm 45) and the sinful (Psalm 69). Ventriloquizing the psalmist's voice also placed Mary in a position where she could directly address tyrants and kings (Psalms 52 and 82), thus confronting and subverting the Pauline strictures against women's preaching and instruction cited above.

The psalms were never printed in Mary's lifetime, but circulated widely in manuscript and were known to many contemporary poets including Daniel, Greville and Jonson. Donne praises the 'Sydnean Psalms' in a commendatory poem that casts Philip and Mary as Moses and Miriam figures, translators of holy learning functioning as the 'organ' for God's divine harmony. Mary wrote two original commendatory poems that preface the psalms in a single manuscript copy which continue to play upon the work's corporate nature. 'To the Angell spirit of the most excellent Sir Phillip Sidney' compares the psalms' unfinished state upon Sidney's death to her brother's own 'maim'd' and bleeding body, but presents the completed 'coupled worke' as the product of their conjoined muses. The second poem, 'Even now that Care which on thy Crowne attends', is addressed to Queen Elizabeth and compares the psalms to a cloth woven from 'stuffe not ours' (i.e. the translated words of other parties) and goes on to contrive an analogy between King David's successful rule and that of the queen. The manuscript containing both poems was probably prepared for presentation to Elizabeth at her proposed visit to Wilton in 1599, as was Mary's rejoinder to Sidney's 1577 pastoral show, her own 'Dialogue between two shepheards, Thenot and Piers, in praise of Astrea'. Mary's deployment of David and Astraea figures proved that she was equally as adroit as her brother at working with the mythographic representational vocabulary of Elizabethan panegyric. The queen never made it to Wilton in 1599 but if she had it is possible that the psalms manuscript could have been used in an attempt to secure the translation royal approval and legitimation prior to publication in print.

Following her husband's death in 1601 Mary's status as a literary patron diminished somewhat, although this aspect of the family tradition was maintained by her son William, later to be Shakespeare's patron. Mary nevertheless remained an important role model for women writers throughout the twenty years of her widowhood, and her work establishes a vital precedent for early modern female authorship, as Daniel implies:

> Great sister of the Muses glorious starre
> Of femall worth, who didst at first disclose
> Vnto our times, what noble powers there are
> In womens harts, and sent example farre
> To call vp others to like studious thoughts.[3]

Aemilia Lanyer praised Mary's scholarly community in her *Salve Deus Rex Judaeorum* (1611). *Antonius* provided Elizabeth Cary with an important model for imitation when writing her own closet drama *The Tragedy of Mariam* (1613). Mary's niece Lady Mary Wroth identifies her as a poet whilst praising her through the figure of the Queen of Naples in the richly allusive *Urania* (1621). Wroth would be equally generous in her play *Love's Victory* (c.1620) when alluding to her aunt's relationship with a young lover, Sir Matthew Lister, through the characters Simeana and Lissius. Mary's achievements, not only in her roles as editor and patron but as translator, poet and literary authority, easily make her the most important female writer of the early seventeenth century.

FULKE GREVILLE

Greville's inscription for his tomb in St Mary's church, Warwick, offers a telling insight into the relationships through which he sought to fashion an identity for himself in both life and death: 'Servant to Queen Elizabeth, Councillor to King James, and Friend to Sir Philip Sidney'. He had a varied, and ultimately successful career as courtier and statesman but it is through his friendship with Sidney that he is now principally remembered. Greville's life and writings are hugely influenced by his friend: he is closely involved in constructing Sidney's posthumous textual image, through both editing the 1590 *Old Arcadia* and penning Sidney's biography; and he also wrote many works of his own that imitated and manipulated forms and traditions used by the Sidney circle. Very little of Greville's poetry circulated widely or was published during his lifetime, which complicates precise dating of works. Nevertheless, he is identified as a poet not only by Puttenham but also by fellow

'Areopagites' Spenser and Harvey in their published correspondence, and his earliest works were composed in concert with the poetic exercises of the Sidney-centred coterie.

Greville's most accessible work is *Caelica* ('heavenly one'), a collection of 109 poems, forty-one of which are fourteen-line sonnets, that he composed and revised throughout his life and which intersect with many of his other writings and the ideas explored therein. *Caelica* is frequently described as a sonnet sequence and discussed alongside representative examples such as *Astrophil* and Spenser's *Amoretti* (1595). However, although individual groupings of poems, recurrent preoccupations and favoured addressees are perceptible, *Caelica* might best be considered an anthology of private responses to the brittle world of early modern court culture as well as to more theological and philosophical issues. The first seventy-six poems (dated 1576–87) adopt many of the Petrarchan conventions for representing the agony and ecstasy of love: Cupid's wanton archery; the beloved's quasi-divinity; the inconstancy of worldly love. *Caelica*'s first 'movement' features many poems addressed to beloved figures named Myra, Cynthia and Caelica, though there is little consistent characterization or biographical allusion. Each is representative more of individual moments of worldly love, as Greville appears to be interested not in a real relationship with a woman but in ideas found in constructing that relationship.[4] Greville does gesture towards the familiar narrative arc of initial worship, unsuccessful pursuit and ultimate rejection in several poems concerning extended absence from Cynthia and Caelica, though the focus is more on the poet's inaction when they are together (e.g. Sonnets 56, 74) and on absence as an abstract concept. Numerous poems in *Caelica* respond to lyrics by Sidney and Spenser: for example, Sonnet 1 employs the same device, *gradatio*, used in Sidney's opening sonnet; Sonnets 13 and 14 address *Astrophil* 17 and 18; and Sonnet 3 echoes *Amoretti* 8.

But Greville is far more explicitly sceptical than his contemporaries towards the commonplaces of amorous verse. The agent of love, Cupid (Greville's most frequent addressee), is repeatedly scorned as being deceitful, inconstant and, at points, a mere idol (Sonnet 62). Women are regularly berated for their fickleness and promiscuity (e.g. Sonnets 30, 50) and *Caelica*'s conventional golden tresses are revealed to be a wig (Sonnet 58). The collection's first section closes with Caelica imploring the poet-figure (named Philocell) to reject his worldly desires:

> Wake yourself from passion's trance,
> And let reason guide affection,
> From despair to new election.
>
> (Gunn, Sonnet 75, ll. 104–6).

References to 'despair' and 'election' have particular resonance here as Greville appropriates Calvinist language, with its focus on mankind's inability to achieve salvation and dependence on divine grace alone, to characterize the lover's inevitable sense of helplessness and frustration. 'Election' is a term used to describe the fortunate state of being predestined for salvation and is played upon earlier in Sonnet 4 to represent the beloved's active choice of the poet as a lover. In the earlier parts of *Caelica*, the use of Calvinist terminology, together with sporadic critiques of worldly love's limitations, anticipates the shift to more serious issues in the final twenty or so poems, affording an often overlooked level of coherence to the collection. Love is thus examined in both its earthly and heavenly forms.

Sonnets 76 and onwards dwell far more on political, religious and philosophical issues, though Greville returns momentarily to amorous complaint, concluding a litany of reflections upon lost joys with a punning reflexive allusion ('Let no man ask my name, nor what else I should be;/ For Greive-Ill, pain, forlorn estate do best decypher me' (Gunn, Sonnet 83, ll. 97–8)), before the following sonnet finally bids Cupid farewell. Greville also presents a quasi-heraldic panegyric on the queen (Sonnet 81) in which he juxtaposes her constancy with the shifting claims of fortune. Critics often explain the shift between the worldly interests of Greville's earlier poetry and the serious tone of the later by suggesting that he experiences a deepening religious conviction following Sidney's death. Marotti challenges this by arguing that Greville switched from love poetry to religious and philosophical themes when the use of amorous verse to express social, economic and political ambition popular at Elizabeth's court lost its 'importance as a cultural idiom' within the Jacobean court.[5]

Greville's political sonnets offer personal meditations on ambition, court favouritism, and tyranny, issues he interrogates further in the closet dramas *Mustapha* and *Alaham* produced around the same time (c.1594–1601). Greville characterizes his plays as political morality dramas written to 'trace out the highways of ambitious governors, and to show in the practice of life that the more audacity, advantage and good success such sovereignties have, the more they hasten to their own desolation and ruin' (Gouws, 133). Both plays use contemporary Middle-Eastern history as the setting in which to demonstrate the fatal consequences of court factionalism and ill counsel (in *Mustapha*) and naked ambition (in *Alaham*). Both are written against the backdrop of the Earl of Essex's rise to power during the 1590s that came to a head in 1601 with an abortive coup, following which Essex was executed. Essex was initially close to the Sidney circle: he married Sidney's widow and was friend to Greville and Robert Sidney. As Leicester's heir, he was also popularly viewed as both militant Protestant rallying-point and Elizabeth's favourite, and appeared to represent the answer to concerns about the royal succession and the aging queen's growing unpopularity. Both plays mirror this situation in vocalizing anxieties felt by courtiers regarding aspiring favourites and weak monarchs. Prudently, Greville never intended to stage his plays (though a pirated *Mustapha* appeared in 1609) and went as far as to burn a play he wrote about Antony and Cleopatra, fearing it should be discovered and read as a controversial commentary on the Essex affair. Disputation forms the bulk of the narrative matter in both extant plays. Greville's characters possess very little depth or interiority but provide a means of juxtaposing contrasting political and moral positions and the choruses in each play offer further opportunity for rehearsing debates. Nevertheless, Greville creates engaging characters in both plays, such as the villainous, transgressive queens Rossa and Hala, who call to mind Medea or Cecropia. Of greatest interest are the 'good counsellor' figures Achmat (from *Mustapha*) and Mahomet (from *Alaham*), whose voices clearly come closest to Greville's own, and who each face the dilemma of having to choose between inciting popular revolt to preserve state interests or acquiesce with the tyrannous status quo. In each case Greville foregrounds political non-resistance and the cultivation instead of inward constancy and patient, spiritual endurance as a response to worldly corruption. This obviously accords with

Neostoic ideas expressed in *Antonius* and is echoed in Greville's other works, including *A Letter to an Honorable Lady* (*c*.1601), in which he counsels constancy and piety to a woman (possibly Margaret Clifford, Countess of Cumberland) being ill-treated by her husband.

In both the closet dramas and *Life of Sidney* (discussed earlier) Greville reveals that he is no less the politician than Sidney, and that he is actually consistently less confrontational and more productive than his friend in his criticism of political institutions. Greville's famous remark 'I know the world and believe in God' exemplifies his view of the relationship between worldly and heavenly order. Whilst his writings reveal a growing scepticism and pessimism about the world, one can still identify his enduring belief in the capacity of correctly ordered temporal institutions and faculties, combined with faith, to shape mankind so that one might play a positive, active role in the postlapsarian world. Nowhere is this more apparent than in Greville's verse treatises on monarchy, fame and honour, wars, human learning and religion, which developed initially, as outlined in the *Life*, as choruses to his plays (Gouws, 90–92). Despite huge variety in scope, each treatise concentrates initially upon the negative, fallen nature of each concept or institution before offering Greville's commentary on its positive manifestation and qualities. The treatises function as guides for working within a fallen world, demonstrating the implications of the fall upon human institutions together with instruction regarding application of laws and injunctions with which to form the 'matter' of mankind anew. Throughout the treatises Greville uses imagery connected with moulding or refining existing fallen material to express the seeming paradox of how one may function productively in the world. Monarchy – correctly constituted – thus offers a framework for organizing the potential chaos of the temporal state. Greville conceives that his writing offers a 'Modell' so that

> wiser men may see,
> That there is choice even in the vanitie
>
> And formes establisht, which must be obay'd,
> As levells for the world to guide her owne,
> Foundations against Anarchie well layd,
> Whose beinge is but beings overthrowne;

> Where Thrones (as mortall shrynes) with mortall feare
> Must be ador'd, and worshipt everie where.
>
> (Wilkes, *Monarchy*, sts 662–3)

Similarly in *A Treatie of Humane Learning* Greville argues that human knowledge focused upon utility rather than delight offers a framework for enacting a form of moral regeneration, offering a far more austere vision of the function of language and rhetoric in a fallen world than Sidney proposes in the *Defence*. In *A Treatise of Religion*, one of his very last writings, Greville upholds the Calvinist position that regeneration through grace comes from God alone but also suggests that mankind should still actively seek to recover God's image through maintaining a selfless life of obedience and godly conduct. Contrary to the utter helplessness predicated by Calvinist doctrine on predestination, Greville continues to believe in the efficacy of temporal actions. Even the pressures of fear and temptation in the world have a positive value in providing the basis for mankind's improvement:

> Then man! Rest on this feelinge from above,
> Plant thou thy faith on this celestiall way.
> The world is made for use; God is for Love;
> Sorrowe for sinne; knowledge, but to obay;
> Feare and temptation, to refine and prove;
> The heaven, for joyes; Desire that it may
> Finde peace in endlesse, boundlesse, heavenly things;
> Place it else where, it desolation bringes.
>
> (Wilkes, *Religion*, st. 114)

Greville echoes such sentiments in the later *Caelica* poems (Sonnets 82, 85–109, written c.1604–28), using his poetry to model a realization both of loss and of God's capacity for providing mercy and spiritual recovery. Such poems are frequently admired for their suggestion of unmediated intimacy, verbal clarity and directness of expression exemplary of the early modern 'plain' style, and for their stark articulation of a Calvinist reflection upon the desolation of the fallen human soul that distinguishes them from work by Greville's confederates. But, as in the verse treatises, Greville identifies a positive function for the world and his writings in the search for salvation. This is best illustrated by Sonnet 99, 'Down in the depth of mine iniquity' (though echoed in Sonnets 98, 100 and 109). Greville alternates here between description of the infernal condition into which one is plunged when considering one's state of sinfulness, and a refrain that changes significantly as the poem progresses, asserting awareness that only when placed in such a state does one realize the redemptive powers of 'this saving God of mine'. By this point Greville has fully reworked the language of Petrarchan lyric for his own personal, religious, meditative purposes. The specular preoccupations of Petrarchanism seen earlier in *Caelica* in repeated references to mirrors, visions and gazes – and possibly alluded to punningly in the sonnet-mistress Myra – are now replaced by an intense impulse towards spiritual self-examination and the search for evidence of divine grace to furnish one's hopes of salvation. Little imagery is deployed here and hell is characterized simply as a state of absence, though Greville emphasizes the growing clarity of an image through which salvation may be achieved: the 'appearance' of God in the first three refrains culminating in the vision of Christ's crucifixion and His atonement for our sins. The penultimate quatrain voices a dawning realization that one may be deprived of human graces but not the divine, whilst the final quatrain reverses the direction of the vertical emphasis established from the poem's first word, and casts the raising of Christ on the cross as the logical means by which one's soul is saved: 'Thus hath his death rais'd up this soul of mine' (Gunn, Sonnet 99, l. 24). Visualization and reflection are key themes within the poem and the means by which the state modelled therein may be transcended by the reader – if only Greville himself – in the world outside. Like a prayer, the very form of Greville's poetry offers a productive, personal means of articulating hope and initiating spiritual recovery.

ROBERT SIDNEY

Robert Sidney lived much of his life in his brother's shadow and it is only relatively recently that his posthumous reputation has been founded as much on his own accomplishments as a poet. His poetry, which was only identified in 1973, offers valuable further insight into the immediate circle of those responding to

Sidney and is another example of how courtier verse was used to voice anxieties about personal and political misfortunes. Robert's poetry exists in a unique autograph manuscript that carries a simple dedication to his sister Mary and was probably all written post-1586, most likely during the late 1590s. The collection consists of sixty-six poems, combining sonnets with songs, pastorals and a single elegy. Like both his siblings, Robert demonstrates an interest in experimenting with a wide variety of forms and metres. There are certainly verbal echoes of Sidney's sonnets in Robert's collection but at no point is he slavishly imitating or reworking his late brother's poetry, nor does he ever really address or respond to individual poems by Sidney to the same extent as Greville and Dyer. Instead, Robert continues to pursue his brother's aims of exploring what may be contemplated and achieved through English verse.

Whilst there is evidence for some kind of established authorial ordering of the collection this is essentially a Petrarchan miscellany that uses many of the conventions seen in *Astrophil* and other contemporary courtly verse to reflect on moments of longing and rejection. Imagery evoking the incendiary nature of love, the cruel servitude of the lover's condition, and the beloved's heavenly qualities is deployed throughout. But in Robert's hands it has a violence and viscerality rarely seen amongst contemporary sonneteers. He compares the necessary distancing of himself from a love that betrays him to amputating one's gangrenous limbs (Sonnet 26), and casts himself as a leper suffering under the pernicious 'Falsehood' (Sonnet 27). Witness also the arresting language and stance of Sonnet 21 used to express the failure of outward forms to communicate his internal pain:

> Alas why say you I am rich? when I
> Do beg, and begging scant a life sustain:
> Why do you say that I am well? – when pain
> Louder than on the rack, in me doth cry.
> O let me know myself! My poverty
> With whitening rotten walls not stay doth gain,
> And these small hopes you tell, keep but in vain
> Life with hot drinks, in one laid down to die.
> If in my face my warts and sores so great
> Do not appear, a canker (think) unseen

> The apple's heart, though sound without, doth eat:
> Or if on me from my fair heaven are seen
> Some scattered beams – know such heat gives their light
> As frosty morning's sun, as moonshine night.
>
> (Croft, Sonnet 21)

Struggles with, and wounds received by love are frequently couched in military or maritime terms (e.g. Sonnets 7, 15, 24) that remind us that much of Robert's verse was the product of garrison conditions endured during his extended service in his brother's old post as Governor of Flushing. Absence is a major theme of the collection and features not only (following convention) as an abstract concept, but as a very real state affecting Robert and his wife Barbara, who was based at the family home at Penshurst and with whom he maintained an extensive correspondence. Biographical identifications are problematic in conventional poetry. There is, however, a genuine affection and longing for a realized beloved in Song 6, which imagines how his wife would react to news of his death through telling the story, based on a traditional ballad, of a pilgrim informing a knight's widow of her husband's death from the pain of absence. The knight specifically locates the lady 'Near Medway's sandy bed' not far from Penshurst (Croft, Song 6, l. 74). Robert's amorous poetry thus had a personal function, offering a momentary retreat from the vicissitudes of the world about him. Elsewhere Robert appears to create a pastoral alter ego for himself, Rosis (akin to Philip's Philisides), who nobly keeps the nymph Lysa warm during cold weather, though, playing on the Petrarchan conceit of the 'icy fire', cannot figure out why his own amorous 'fires' fail to offer warmth (Pastoral 7).

Whereas there was a wittiness and levity to *Astrophil*, even at the points at which the lover is rebuffed, Robert's poetry remains consistently melancholic in tone and preoccupied with betrayal and the changing of one's fortunes. It is therefore often suggested that Robert uses the sense of powerlessness that becomes the Petrarchan lover to meditate upon his own perceived political failings during the later part of Elizabeth's reign. Poetry offered Robert a means of contemplating his increasingly stalled career during the bleak demi-exile of his Netherlands posting, and how time seemed to be passing him by (see Sonnet 35). Robert's fortunes did change during James's reign, and thereafter he returned to England more frequently and acquired a series of titles until made Earl of Leicester in 1618. Robert's interest and skill in music was often noted by his contemporaries and he appears to have been involved in musical settings of some of his poetry. Jonson celebrated the Sidney household in his poem 'To Penshurst' praising Robert as a patron and head of a cultured family. In the same poetry collection, *The Forest*, Jonson also praised the poetic accomplishments of Sidney's daughter Elizabeth, Countess of Rutland. Like his brother, Robert had interests in courtly entertainments and, as Lord Chamberlain to Queen Anne, organized several court masques scripted by Jonson in which his daughter Lady Mary Wroth participated.

LADY MARY WROTH

Like her uncle Philip Sidney, Lady Mary Wroth had great expectations. She was born into a family with a tremendous political and literary heritage and like her aunt (after whom she was named) would continue to use the Sidney name as the basis for fashioning her own identity as a writer. During her youth she distinguished herself in learning and writing and was also praised for her dancing and musical talents. At the age of 17 she was married to Sir Robert Wroth, an Essex landowner popular with the king who often entertained James on his estates. Again like her aunt, Mary Wroth retained the Sidney coat of arms when married but also sought a form of autonomy from her husband through consciously asserting her sanguineous family connections. The title page of her romance *Urania* proudly displays the relations through which she identifies herself: 'daughter to the Right Noble Robert Earl of Leicester, and niece to the ever-famous and renowned Sir Philip Sidney, Knight, and to that most exalted Lady Mary, Countess of Pembroke, late deceased' (Roberts, 76). The Sidney heritage offered refuge from what seems from the outset to have been an unhappy marriage. Whilst her husband preferred hunting in Essex, Wroth was closely involved in Jacobean court culture, participating in masques and entertainments and being celebrated in her own right as a patron. Jonson dedicated *The Alchemist* to her in 1612 and praises her literary endeavours. Wroth's husband died in 1614, saddling her with huge amounts of debt. Wroth was also by this time engaged in an affair with her cousin William Herbert and they ultimately had two illegitimate children together. The affair's scandal, possibly combined with the fact that the philandering Herbert was also a favourite of Queen Anne, saw Wroth dismissed from court.

Withdrawal from court provided Wroth with the occasion to write her romance *The Countess of Montgomery's Urania*, which was probably started around 1618 and dedicated to her friend, Herbert's sister-in-law. Chivalric romance had long been associated with female readers and dedicatees, as signalled in the title of *The Countess of Pembroke's Arcadia*, and the feared effeminacy of the form haunts Sidney's work. But *Urania* goes a stage further in being the first romance written both for and by a woman. It is a vast, encyclopaedic work, consisting of a first part, which was published in 1621 (encompassing 558 folio pages) accompanied by a sonnet sequence *Pamphilia to Amphilanthus*, and an unfinished second instalment in manuscript. The romance and sonnet genres were both rather unfashionable by this time but they provided Wroth with a means of signalling an affinity with, and continuation of the Sidney literary 'brand'. There are numerous echoes of characters and episodes from the *New Arcadia* in *Urania*, Wroth's title itself alluding back to the mysterious shepherdess lamented by Klaius and Strephon. Urania is given voice at the opening of Wroth's romance as she complains of her anxiety about establishing her place and identity in the world. *Urania* draws on many of the commonplaces of chivalric romance – knights, quests, enchantments, villainous enemies and numerous damsels in distress – and, alongside the *Arcadias*, evokes both the Hellenistic and native romance traditions. Wroth's characters visit symbolic locations that recall those of Spenser's *Faerie Queene*, such as the Palace of Love on Venus's island, in which many lovers find themselves imprisoned, and the Hell of Deceit, a Petrarchan torture chamber representing the delusions of false love.

What makes *Urania* distinct – and original – is that Wroth goes far further than Sidney or Spenser in foregrounding female conceptions of virtue, exploring the psychological state of female characters in romance and constructing a mode of female heroism centred on constancy. *Urania*'s narrative is far more complex than that of either *Arcadia*, but one of the central strands is the love of Queen Pamphilia ('all-loving') for the fickle Amphilanthus ('lover of two'). Throughout many convoluted plots and interpolated stories Wroth charts Pamphilia's dogged constancy in her loyalty to Amphilanthus despite the latter's chequered past and frequent transgressions. Pamphilia's constancy indeed provides a landmark for the reader as they work their way through the romance's sprawling, chaotic landscape. She is a model against which repeated instances of male inconstancy in love may be measured. Wroth thus inverts the traditional female stereotype found extensively in amorous poetry concerning the fickleness of women. Wroth also adopts this inverted stance in her related sequence *Pamphilia to Amphilanthus*, appropriating the traditionally male rhetorical power to construct and ventriloquize a mute subject found in Petrarchan verse. But the sequence is more subtle than a simple role reversal. Wroth is initially reliant on Petrarchan conventions to anatomize the vicissitudes of Pamphilia's constant affections for the capricious Amphilanthus. Wroth differs, however, from many male sonneteers in that she rarely emphasizes Amphilanthus's physical presence. Instead the sequence is clearly presented as a personal, reflective mechanism for contemplating an idealized love, rather than the means through which Pamphilia actively woos her beloved. Towards the sequence's close Wroth explores the 'strange labyrinth' of love through the device of a crown of fourteen sonnets – in which the first line of each poem repeats the final line of that preceding – beginning with confusion and disorientation but slowly realizing that love must be counselled by reason and truth. As in *Urania* as a whole, Wroth casts constancy as the answer to temporal insecurity and changeability. The final poem, Sonnet 103, draws a distinction largely absent in earlier sequences between the sportive love that is the 'discource of Venus, and her sunn' and the productive force that binds a constant, faithful relationship (Roberts, 142).

Pamphilia ultimately marries someone else at the very end of *Urania*, though Amphilanthus finally appears to have been schooled in the virtue of chaste constancy and it is suggested that the former lovers and Pamphilia's new husband will live together in an entirely honourable *ménage à trois*. Despite

Pamphilia's rule and the numerous female characters Wroth introduces, this is still very much a patriarchal landscape peopled by domineering fathers and abusive husbands. Examples abound of the unhappiness generated by forced marriages, creating love triangles of lover, beloved and spouse such as that of Perissus, Limena and her violent husband. As Wroth's own experience confirmed, dynastic families could provide security and stability but were also potentially the source of great tragedy, hurt or infamy.

Pamphilia is not only a lover and queen, she is also a writer and storyteller and throughout *Urania* she is seen committing her feelings and anxieties to poetry as did the Arcadian lovers. Indeed Amphilanthus learns of Pamphilia's true feelings when he discovers and reads her impassioned verse. In this regard Pamphilia represents one of the ways in which Wroth creates an autobiographical persona for herself in her work, and there is little subtlety in her portrait of Pamphilia's womanizing cousin Amphilanthus, patently a figure for Herbert. When reading *Urania* one soon becomes aware of the extent to which the text functions as an extensive *roman-à-clef* through which Wroth projects, reflects and meditates on figures and events from the Jacobean courtly and aristocratic spheres, maintaining an allusive literary engagement with the public world which she was denied. Further figures of Wroth appear in Bellamira and Lindamira, the former burdened with a husband obsessed with hunting, the latter victimized by a jealous queen. The marriage of Lindamira's father Bersindor to 'a great Heyre' brings to mind that of Wroth's parents. Wroth's often satiric innuendos were soon identified by her contemporaries following *Urania*'s publication and nobleman Edward Denny, Baron Waltham, was hugely offended by allusions to his family in the transparent Seralius episode which features a father nearly murdering his daughter as punishment for adultery. Denny attacked the wider concept of female authorship itself calling Wroth a 'Hermaphrodite' who should 'leave idle bookes alone/ For wise and worthyer women have written none'.[6] Wroth mounted a spirited epistolary defence but was forced to withdraw *Urania* from circulation. Part 2 of *Urania* thus remained in manuscript but continues in much the same vein as part 1. The familial emphasis remains though Wroth now focuses on the children of part 1's heroes and heroines, and the older characters take on more public roles as counsellors of the next generation. Part 2 also provided narrative materials for Wroth's pastoral closet drama *Love's Victory*, yet another demonstration of her expansion of the generic range of women's writing in this period. The play, loosely derived from Petrarch's *Triumph of Love*, shows the triumph of Venus and Cupid over the hearts of four rustic couples, each of which alludes to amorous pairings from amongst Wroth's family and friends.

Wroth proved herself a worthy heir of the Sidney cultural legacy through her continued innovations in literary form, her use of literary texts to explore issues of gender, court politics and personal virtue, and her creation of fictional personae and landscapes through which to comment upon the interpenetration of private and public life. She also built on her aunt's achievements in continuing to expand the imaginative scope of seventeenth-century women's writing.

Notes

CHAPTER 1. THE COURTLY PERFORMER

1. Roger Howell, *Sir Philip Sidney: The Shepherd Knight* (Boston: Little, Brown, 1968), 11.
2. Alan Stewart, *Sir Philip Sidney: A Double Life* (London: Chatto and Windus, 2000), 34.
3. Ibid., 163–4.
4. Ibid., 94.
5. Catherine Bates, *The Rhetoric of Courtship in Elizabethan Language and Literature* (Cambridge: Cambridge University Press, 1992), 2–3.
6. Steven W. May, *The Elizabethan Courtier Poets: The Poems and Their Contexts* (Asheville, NC: Pegasus Press, 1999), 31.
7. Sir Thomas Wilson, *The Arte of Rhetoric*, ed. Peter Medine (University Park, PA: Pennsylvania State University Press, 1994), 210.
8. Stephen Greenblatt, *Renaissance Self-Fashioning: From More to Shakespeare* (Chicago: University of Chicago Press, 1980), 162.
9. Gavin Alexander (ed.), *Sidney's 'The Defence of Poesy' and Selected Renaissance Literary Criticism* (London: Penguin, 2004), 159.
10. See J. W. Saunders, 'The Stigma of Print: A Note on the Social Bases of Tudor Poetry', *Essays in Criticism*, 1 (1954), 139–64; Colin Burrow, *Edmund Spenser* (Plymouth: Northcote House, 1996); Jean R. Brink, 'Manuscript Culture Revisited', *Sidney Journal*, 17:1 (1999), 19–30.
11. Alexander, *Sidney's 'The Defence of Poesy'*, 105.
12. Ibid., 89.

CHAPTER 2. ARCADIAN TOYS

1. Katherine Duncan-Jones, *Sir Philip Sidney, Courtier Poet* (London: Hamish Hamilton, 1991), 142.
2. Roger Ascham, *Toxophilus*, ed. Peter Medine (Tempe, AZ: ACMRS,

2003), 41.
3. There is also record of Sidney reading *The Old Arcadia* aloud to his friend the exiled Earl of Angus in 1582; see Dorothy Connell, *Sir Philip Sidney: The Maker's Mind* (Oxford: Clarendon Press, 1977), 80.
4. Stewart, *Sir Philip Sidney*, 230.
5. Mary Ellen Lamb, *Gender and Authorship in the Sidney Circle* (Madison: University of Wisconsin Press, 1990), 83.
6. David Norbrook, *Poetry and Politics in the English Renaissance* (Oxford: Oxford University Press, 2002), 85.
7. Andrew King, 'Sidney and Spenser', in *A Companion to Romance: From Classical to Contemporary*, ed. Corinne Saunders (Oxford: Blackwell, 2004), 143.
8. Blair Worden, *The Sound of Virtue: Sir Philip Sidney's 'Arcadia' and Elizabethan Politics* (New Haven: Yale University Press, 1996), 4.

CHAPTER 3. THEORY AND PRACTICE

1. Alexander, *Sidney's 'The Defence of Poesy'*, xxxi–xxxii, lx.
2. Quoted in Peter C. Herman (ed.), *Sir Philip Sidney's 'An Apology for Poetry' and 'Astrophil and Stella': Texts and Contexts* (Glen Allen, VA: College Publishing, 2001), 223.
3. Quoted in Alan Sinfield, *Faultlines: Cultural Materialism and the Politics of Dissident Reading* (Oxford: Clarendon Press, 1992), 185.
4. See Andrew Weiner, *Sir Philip Sidney and the Poetics of Protestantism* (Minneapolis: University of Minnesota Press, 1978), 147–85; Margaret Dana, 'The Providential Plot of the *Old Arcadia*', in *Sir Philip Sidney: An Anthology of Modern Criticism*, ed. Dennis Kay (Oxford: Clarendon Press, 1987), 83–102.
5. John Calvin, *Institutes of the Christian Religion*, trans. Henry Beveridge (2 vols; London: James Clarke, 1962), ii. 233–5 (book 2, chapter 2.12–13).

CHAPTER 4. *ASTROPHIL AND STELLA*

1. Quoted in Dennis Kay, 'Introduction: Sidney – A Critical Heritage', in Kay (ed.), *Sir Philip Sidney*, 12.
2. Maurice Evans (ed.), *Elizabethan Sonnets* (London: Dent, 1994), xviii–xix.
3. Richard Helgerson, *The Elizabethan Prodigals* (Berkeley: University of California Press, 1976), 144.
4. Alexander, *Sidney's 'The Defence of Poesy'*, 104.
5. Edward Berry, *The Making of Sir Philip Sidney* (Toronto: University of

Toronto Press, 1998), 103.
6. C. S. Lewis, *English Literature in the Sixteenth Century* (Oxford: Clarendon Press, 1954), 491.
7. Arthur Marotti, '"Love Is Not Love": Elizabethan Sonnet Sequences and the Social Order', *ELH*, 49 (1982), 396–428.
8. Gary F. Waller, 'The Rewriting of Petrarch: Sidney and the Languages of Sixteenth-Century Poetry', in *Sir Philip Sidney and the Interpretation of Renaissance Culture*, ed. Gary F. Waller and Michael D. Moore (London: Croom Helm, 1984), 70.
9. Alan Sinfield, *Literature in Protestant England, 1560–1660* (London: Croom Helm, 1983), 59.
10. Arthur Marotti, *Manuscript, Print and the English Renaissance Lyric* (Ithaca: Cornell University Press, 1995), 229.

CHAPTER 5. REFASHIONINGS

1. William A. Ringler (ed.), *The Poems of Sir Philip Sidney* (Oxford: Clarendon Press, 1962), 376–7.
2. S. K. Heninger, *Sidney and Spenser: The Poet as Maker* (London: Pennsylvania State University Press, 1989), 490–93.
3. Patricia Parker, *Inescapable Romance: Studies in the Poetics of a Mode* (Princeton: Princeton University Press, 1979), 6.
4. John Hoskins, *Directions for Speech and Style*, ed. Hoyt H. Hudson (Princeton: Princeton University Press, 1935), 47.
5. H. R. Woudhuysen, *Sir Philip Sidney and the Circulation of Manuscripts, 1558–1640* (Oxford: Clarendon Press, 1996), 220–21.
6. Quoted in Stewart, *Sir Philip Sidney*, 320.
7. George Whetstone, *Sir Philip Sidney, his honorable life, his valiant death, and his true vertues* (London, 1587), sig. A4v.
8. Lisa Richardson, 'Elizabeth in Arcadia: Fulke Greville and John Hayward's Construction of Elizabeth, 1610–12', in *The Myth of Elizabeth*, ed. Susan Doran and Thomas S. Freeman (Basingstoke: Palgrave Macmillan, 2003), 99–119.
9. Joel Davis, 'Multiple Arcadias and the Literary Quarrel Between Fulke Greville and the Countess of Pembroke', *Studies in Philology*, 101 (2004), 401–30.

CHAPTER 6. THE SIDNEY CIRCLE

1. Lamb, *Gender and Authorship in the Sidney Circle*, 140.
2. Beth Wynne Fisken, '"The Art of Sacred Parody" in Mary Sidney's *Psalmes*', *Tulsa Studies in Women's Literature*, 8 (1989), 227.

3. Dedication to *Cleopatra* in Samuel Daniel, *Certaine small workes* (London, 1611), sig. E3r.
4. Helen Vincent, "'Syon Lies Waste'': Secularity, Scepticism and Religion in *Caelica*', *Sidney Journal*, 19 (2001), 66.
5. Marotti, "'Love Is Not Love'", 420.
6. Lamb, *Gender and Authorship in the Sidney Circle*, 157.

Select Bibliography

SIR PHILIP SIDNEY

Modern Editions

The Correspondence of Sir Philip Sidney and Hubert Languet, ed. S. A. Pears (London, 1846; repr. New York: Gregg, 1971). More for the specialist but contains a wealth of engaging insights into Sidney's intellectual development.

The Complete Works of Sir Philip Sidney, ed. A. Feuillerat (4 vols; Cambridge: Cambridge University Press, 1912–26). Includes first modern edition of the *Old Arcadia*. Reissued in 1962 and still widely cited although the textual editing has now been revealed to be flawed in many places. Volume 3 contains a selection of Sidney's letters.

The Poems of Sir Philip Sidney, ed. William A. Ringler (Oxford: Clarendon Press, 1962). Definitive critical edition, includes informative appendices on Sidneian verse forms, adaptations, musical settings and the appearance of Sidney's poetry in early modern anthologies.

The Psalms of Sir Philip Sidney and the Countess of Pembroke, ed. J. C. A. Rathmell (New York: New York University Press, 1963). Includes short contextual introduction but little annotation.

An Apology for Poetry or The Defence of Poesy, ed. Geoffrey Shepherd (London, 1965; revd edn R. W. Maslen, Manchester: Manchester University Press, 2002). The most detailed critical edition of the *Defence*.

The Countess of Pembroke's Arcadia, intro. Carl Dennis (Kent, OH: Kent State University Press, 1970). Facsimile edition of the 1590 *Arcadia*.

Miscellaneous Prose of Sir Philip Sidney, ed. Katherine Duncan-Jones and Jan van Dorsten (Oxford: Clarendon Press, 1973). Contains the *Defence of Leicester*, 'Discourse on Irish Affairs' and *Letter to the Queen*.

The Countess of Pembroke's Arcadia (The Old Arcadia), ed. Jean Robertson (Oxford: Clarendon Press, 1973). Scholarly critical edition.

The Countess of Pembroke's Arcadia, ed. Maurice Evans (Harmondsworth:

Penguin, 1977). Modernized student edition of the *New Arcadia*.
The Old Arcadia, ed. Katherine Duncan-Jones (Oxford: Oxford University Press, 1985; reissued 1994). Student edition based on a corrected version of Robertson's *Old Arcadia* text.
The Countess of Pembroke's Arcadia (The New Arcadia), ed. Victor Skretkowicz (Oxford: Clarendon Press, 1987). Scholarly critical edition with comprehensive apparatus.
Elizabethan Sonnets, ed. Maurice Evans (2nd edn, London: Dent, 1994). Most useful student collection of sonnet sequences, includes *Astrophil* and Lady Mary Wroth's *Pamphilia to Amphilanthus*.
Sir Philip Sidney's 'An Apology for Poetry' and 'Astrophil and Stella': Texts and Contexts, ed. Peter C. Herman (Glen Allen, VA: College Publishing, 2001). Also contains a selection of classical and early modern primary materials on the debate surrounding the nature and function of imaginative literature.
Sir Philip Sidney: The Major Works, ed. Katherine Duncan-Jones (2nd edn, Oxford: Oxford University Press, 2002). Includes *The Lady of May*, *Defence, Astrophil, Certain Sonnets* and *Four Foster Children of Desire*.
Sidney's 'The Defence of Poesy' and Selected Renaissance Literary Criticism, ed. Gavin Alexander (London: Penguin, 2004). Contains the *Defence* in addition to poetic treatises by Puttenham, Daniel and Gascoigne.

Biographies and Reference Works

Brennan, Michael G., and Noel J. Kinnamon, *A Sidney Chronology, 1554–1654* (Basingstoke: Palgrave Macmillan, 2003). Month-by-month chronological survey of the literary, political and personal history of Philip, Mary and Robert Sidney, and Lady Mary Wroth.
Buxton, John, *Sir Philip Sidney and the English Renaissance* (2nd edn, London: Macmillan, 1964). Study of Sidney's patronage and relations with Elizabethan men and women of letters. Also includes a chapter on Mary Sidney.
Donow, H. S., *A Concordance to the Poems of Sir Philip Sidney* (Ithaca: Cornell University Press, 1975).
Duncan-Jones, Katherine, *Sir Philip Sidney: Courtier Poet* (London: Hamish Hamilton, 1991). Accessible treatment of Sidney's life and works, though asserts a rigid distinction between the public and private aspects of both.
Garrett, Martin (ed.), *Sir Philip Sidney: The Critical Heritage* (London: Routledge, 1996). Invaluable collection of references and critical responses to Sidney's work written from the sixteenth century onwards.
Howell, Roger, *Sir Philip Sidney: The Shepherd Knight* (Boston: Little, Brown, 1968). Provides information on historical context more than

critical discussion of the literary works.

Moffet, Thomas, *Nobilis, Or, A View of the Life and Death of a Sidney*, ed. and trans. V. B. Heltzel and H. H. Hudson (San Marino: Huntington Library, 1940). Modern edition of the biography written for Sidney's nephew.

Osborn, James M., *Young Philip Sidney, 1572–1577* (New Haven: Yale University Press, 1972). Focuses on Sidney's early continental travels and intellectual connections drawing on previously unpublished correspondence.

Stewart, Alan, *Sir Philip Sidney: A Double Life* (London: Chatto and Windus, 2000). Engaging study focusing on the disparity between Sidney's reputation in England and on the continent.

Stump, Donald V., et al., *Sir Philip Sidney: An Annotated Bibliography of Texts and Criticism (1554–1984)* (New York: Hall, 1994).

Van Dorsten, Jan, *Poets, Patrons and Professors: Sir Philip Sidney, Daniel Rogers and the Leiden Humanists* (Leiden: Brill, 1962). Like Buxton, concentrates on Sidney's continental connections and role as patron.

Wallace, M. W., *The Life of Sir Philip Sidney* (Cambridge: Cambridge University Press, 1915). Still one of the most comprehensive life studies. Largely avoids the whimsy and narrative clichés of many early Sidney biographies.

See also Gouws, John (ed.), *The Prose Works of Fulke Greville* (Oxford: Clarendon Press, 1986), below, for Greville's *Life of Sidney*, also known as *A Dedication to Sir Philip Sidney* (London, 1652).

Essay Collections

Allen, M. J. B. (ed.), *Sir Philip Sidney's Achievements* (New York: AMS Press, 1990). Also includes essays on Mary Sidney and the Sidney legend.

Kay, Dennis (ed.), *Sir Philip Sidney: An Anthology of Modern Criticism* (Oxford: Clarendon Press, 1987). Includes a comprehensive survey of Sidney's critical heritage from the sixteenth century to the mid-twentieth century and a check-list of early editions of Sidney's writings.

Kinney, Arthur F. (ed.), *Essential Articles for the Study of Sir Philip Sidney* (Hamden, CT: Archon, 1986).

—— (ed.), *Sidney in Retrospect* (Amherst: University of Massachusetts Press, 1988). Collection of essays on Sidney's life and writings previously published in the journal *English Literary Renaissance*, 1972–83.

Van Dorsten, Jan, et al. (eds), *Sir Philip Sidney: 1586 and the Creation of a*

Legend (Leiden: Brill, 1986). Strong focus on Sidney's life and posthumous reputation.

Waller, Gary F., and Michael D. Moore (eds), *Sir Philip Sidney and the Interpretation of Renaissance Culture* (London: Croom Helm, 1984). Divided between essays on Sidney's influences within his own lifetime and on his place within modern scholarship.

Criticism

Berry, Edward, *The Making of Sir Philip Sidney* (Toronto: University of Toronto Press, 1998). Concentrates on the fictional selves Sidney fashions for himself through his writings.

Connell, Dorothy, *Sir Philip Sidney: The Maker's Mind* (Oxford: Clarendon Press, 1977). On Sidney's conception of what it meant to be a poet and to write about love.

Davis, Walter, and Richard A. Lanham, *Sidney's Arcadia* (New Haven: Yale University Press, 1965). Two separate works bound together. The first, Davis's *A Map of Arcadia: Sidney's Romance in Its Tradition*, treats the *Old Arcadia*'s literary heritage; the second, Lanham's *The Old Arcadia*, offers a more detailed discussion of genre, theme and structure.

Ferguson, Margaret W., *Trials of Desire: Renaissance Defenses of Poetry* (New Haven: Yale University Press, 1983). Examines Sidney's poetic treatise alongside those of Tasso and Joachim du Bellay.

Greenblatt, Stephen, 'Sidney's *Arcadia* and the Mixed Mode', *Studies in Philology*, 70 (1973), 269–78. Maintains that Sidney's conscious cultivation of generic instability in the revised *Arcadia* reflects the instability of human life and modes of conduct.

Hamilton, A. C., *Sir Philip Sidney: A Study of His Life and Works* (Cambridge: Cambridge University Press, 1977). Survey of Sidney's life as a writer, his sources, forms and theories on poetics.

Hardison, O. B., Jr, 'The Two Voices of Sidney's *Apology for Poetry*', *English Literary Renaissance*, 2 (1972), 83–99; reprinted in Kinney (ed.), *Sidney in Retrospect*, 45–61. Argues that Sidney initially writes the *Defence* as a humanist response to Gosson; then begins to revise it in line with more neoclassical ideas on form and genre.

Helgerson, Richard, *The Elizabethan Prodigals* (Berkeley: University of California Press, 1976). Includes a chapter relating Sidney to an authorial model based on rebellion and reproval identified in the 'new' generation of later Elizabethan writers.

Heninger, S. K., *Sidney and Spenser: The Poet as Maker* (London: Pennsylvania State University Press, 1989). Comprehensive study of Sidney and Spenser's conception of imitation and its application in their poetry.

Jones, Ann R., and Peter Stallybrass, 'The Politics of *Astrophil and Stella*', *Studies in English Literature*, 24 (1984), 53–68. Engaging account of Sidney's sequence pursuing a similar political line to that of Marotti's earlier article (see below).

Kalstone, David, *Sidney's Poetry: Contexts and Interpretations* (Cambridge, MA: Harvard University Press, 1965). Pays particular attention to Sidney's relation to pastoral and Petrarchan traditions.

Kimbrough, Robert, *Sir Philip Sidney* (New York: Twayne, 1971). Useful basic overview of Sidney's life and works.

King, Andrew, 'Sidney and Spenser', in *A Companion to Romance: From Classical to Contemporary*, ed. Corinne Saunders (Oxford: Blackwell, 2004), 140–59. Discusses Sidney's evolving conception of romance and its relation to historical events surrounding the Anjou match.

Klein, Lisa M., *The Exemplary Sidney and the Elizabethan Sonneteer* (Newark, NJ: University of Delaware Press, 1998). Addresses how Sidney served as an authoritative model for sonnet sequences by Greville, Daniel and Spenser.

Kuin, Roger, *Chamber Music: Elizabethan Sonnet-Sequences and the Pleasure of Criticism* (Toronto: University of Toronto Press, 1998). Complex, playful, theoretically inflected study of sonnet sequences concentrating on Sidney, Shakespeare and Spenser. Thoughtful and original though perhaps not for the beginner.

——, 'Querre-Muhau: Sir Philip Sidney and the New World', *Renaissance Quarterly*, 51 (1998), 549–85. On Sidney's extended interests in geopolitics and the New World.

Lewis, C. S., *English Literature in the Sixteenth Century* (Oxford: Clarendon Press, 1954). Includes a chapter on Sidney, though Lewis's dogmatic pronouncements on mid-century verse should be read with caution.

Mack, Michael, *Sidney's Poetics: Imitating Creation* (Washington, DC: Catholic University of America Press, 2004). Explores Sidney's conception of the poet's god-like creative powers.

Marotti, Arthur, '"Love Is Not Love": Elizabethan Sonnet Sequences and the Social Order', *ELH*, 49 (1982), 396–428. Seminal discussion of sonnet sequences' social and political bases.

May, Steven W., *The Elizabethan Courtier Poets: The Poems and Their Contexts* (Asheville, NC: Pegasus Press, 1999). Contextual study of courtier verse that treats Sidney and Greville at length.

McCoy, Richard A., *Sir Philip Sidney: Rebellion in Arcadia* (Brighton: Harvester Press, 1979). Nuanced examination of the idea of rebellion in the *Arcadias* and *Astrophil* arguing that Sidney's works explore the balance between sovereignty and autonomy.

Montrose, Louis Adrian, 'Celebration and Insinuation: Sir Philip Sidney and the Motives of Elizabethan Courtship', *Renaissance Drama* n.s. 8

(1977), 3–35. Complex examination of how the language of desire is used to both celebrate and persuade Elizabeth in *The Lady of May*.

——, 'Of Gentlemen and Shepherds: The Politics of Elizabethan Pastoral Form', *ELH*, 50 (1983), 415–59. Discusses how pastoral provides an apposite form through which to voice disaffection at Elizabeth's court.

Montgomery, R. L., *Symmetry and Sense: The Poetry of Sir Philip Sidney* (Austin: University of Texas Press, 1961). Detailed stylistic study concentrating on form and rhetoric more than content and context.

Myrick, Kenneth, *Sir Philip Sidney as a Literary Craftsman* (2nd edn, Lincoln, NE: University of Nebraska Press, 1965). Strong on Sidney's use of classical and contemporary models of oratory and genre. Appendix includes detailed plot summary of both *Arcadias*.

Norbrook, David, *Poetry and Politics in the English Renaissance* (Oxford: Oxford University Press, 2002). Includes a chapter on the politics of Sidneian pastoral.

Patterson, Annabel, *Censorship and Interpretation* (Madison: University of Wisconsin Press, 1984). Includes a chapter examining Sidney's use of pastoral as a form of self-censorship.

Raitière, Martin N., *'Faire bitts': Sir Philip Sidney and Renaissance Political Theory* (Pittsburgh: Duquesne University Press, 1984). Locates Sidney in relation to militant Protestant ideology, particularly in the *Old Arcadia*.

Rees, Joan, *Sir Philip Sidney and Arcadia* (London: Associated University Presses, 1991). Thematic introduction to the *Arcadias*, showing a preference for the revised version.

Robinson, Forrest G., *The Shape of Things Known: Sidney's 'Apology' in Its Philosophical Tradition* (Cambridge, MA: Harvard University Press, 1972). Detailed study on the philosophical and aesthetic terminology and workings of Sidney's treatise.

Roche, Thomas P., *Petrarch and the English Sonnet Sequences* (New York: AMS Press, 1989). Extensive treatment of how English sonneteers (Sidney included) imitate and adapt Petrarchan images and themes.

Rudenstine, Neil L., *Sidney's Poetic Development* (Cambridge, MA: Harvard University Press, 1967). Insists on a continuity of purpose and technique across all of Sidney's writings.

Sinfield, Alan, *Faultlines: Cultural Materialism and the Politics of Dissident Reading* (Oxford: Clarendon Press, 1992). Includes a chapter that expands on Sinfield's earlier work (in *Literature in Protestant England, 1560–1660* (London: Croom Helm, 1983)) arguing that Sidney attempts to integrate the humanist thrust of his writings with a militant Protestant agenda.

Waller, Gary, *English Poetry of the Sixteenth Century* (London: Longman, 1986). Immensely engaging and sophisticated period survey that treats Sidney and the Sidney circle at length.

Weiner, Andrew, *Sir Philip Sidney and the Poetics of Protestantism* (Minneapolis: University of Minnesota, 1978). Argues that Sidney establishes and sustains a committed Protestant conception of poetics throughout his works.

Worden, Blair, *The Sound of Virtue: Sir Philip Sidney's 'Arcadia' and Elizabethan Politics* (New Haven: Yale University Press, 1996). Extensive study of the political background to the *Old Arcadia*.

Woudhuysen, H. R., *Sir Philip Sidney and the Circulation of Manuscripts, 1558–1640* (Oxford: Clarendon Press, 1996). Provides a detailed examination of manuscript circulation before exploring the textual history of Sidney's work in manuscript.

Zandvoort, R. W., *Sidney's Arcadia: A Comparison Between the Two Versions* (Amsterdam: Swets and Zeitlinger, 1929; reissued Folcroft, PA: Folcroft Press, 1969). Still one of the best comparative surveys.

THE SIDNEY CIRCLE

General Studies

Alexander, Gavin, *Writing After Sidney: The Literary Response to Sir Philip Sidney* (Oxford: Oxford University Press, 2006). Focuses on the forms and contexts of Sidney's literary legacy and includes chapters on Mary and Robert Sidney, Greville and Lady Mary Wroth.

Brennan, Michael G., *Literary Patronage in the Renaissance: The Pembroke Family* (London: Routledge, 1988). Uses the extended Sidney–Herbert family as a case study for discussing early modern patronage.

——, *The Sidneys of Penshurst and the Monarchy, 1500–1700* (Aldershot: Ashgate, 2006). Engaging study of the Sidney dynasty's continuing relationship with the Tudor and Stuart monarchy.

Lamb, Mary Ellen, *Gender and Authorship in the Sidney Circle* (Madison: University of Wisconsin Press, 1990). On the importance of Mary Sidney and her circle for the development of women's patronage and writing in the early modern period.

Lewalski, Barbara, *Writing Women in Jacobean England* (Cambridge, MA: Harvard University Press, 1994). Excellent sections on Mary Sidney and Lady Mary Wroth.

Mazzola, Elizabeth, *Favorite Sons: The Politics and Poetics of the Sidney Family* (Basingstoke: Palgrave Macmillan, 2003). Examines Sidney's poetic legacy for his family and the recurrent theme of familial bonds in works of the Sidney circle.

Mary Sidney Herbert, Countess of Pembroke

Cerasano, S. P., and Marion Wynne-Davies (eds), *Renaissance Drama by Women: Texts and Documents* (London: Routledge, 1996). Includes Mary Sidney's *Antonius* and Lady Mary Wroth's *Love's Victory*.

Clark, Danielle (ed.), *Isabella Whitney, Mary Sidney, and Aemilia Lanyer: Renaissance Women Poets* (London: Penguin, 2000). Accessible selection of Mary's work situated alongside that of contemporary early modern women writers.

Fisken, Beth Wynne, '"The Art of Sacred Parody" in Mary Sidney's *Psalmes'*, *Tulsa Studies in Women's Literature*, 8 (1989), 223–39. Valuable exposition of the creativity and boldness of Mary's continuation of the metrical psalms.

Hannay, Margaret P., *Philip's Phoenix: Mary Sidney, Countess of Pembroke* (Oxford: Oxford University Press, 1990). Biographical and critical study.

—— (ed.), *Silent but for the Word: Tudor Women as Patrons, Translators, and Writers of Religious Works* (Kent, OH: Kent State University Press, 1985). Excellent study of early modern women's different authorial models and literary roles.

——, Noel J. Kinnamon and Michael G. Brennan (eds), *The Collected Works of Mary Sidney Herbert, Countess of Pembroke* (2 vols; Oxford: Clarendon Press, 1998). Definitive scholarly edition.

Pritchard, R. E. (ed.), *Mary Sidney: The Sidney Psalms* (Manchester: Carcanet, 1992). Student edition with good introduction but little annotation.

Waller, Gary, *Mary Sidney, Countess of Pembroke: A Critical Study of Her Writings and Literary Milieu* (Salzburg: University of Salzburg, 1979). Biographical and critical account.

Fulke Greville, Lord Brooke

Bullough, Geoffrey (ed.), *Poems and Dramas of Fulke Greville, First Lord Brooke* (2 vols; Edinburgh: Oliver and Boyd, 1939). Still one of the most useful scholarly editions of Greville's works.

Gouws, John (ed.), *The Prose Works of Fulke Greville* (Oxford: Clarendon Press, 1986). Includes the *Life of Sidney* and *A Letter to An Honourable Lady*.

Gunn, Thom (ed.), *Selected Poems of Fulke Greville* (London: Faber, 1968). Also contains a useful, comprehensive introduction to Greville's poetry.

Hansen, Matthew C., and Matthew Woodcock (eds), *Fulke Greville: A Special Double Issue, Sidney Journal*, 19:1 and 2 (2001). Contains new essays on all of Greville's writings.

Ho, Elaine Y. L., 'Fulke Greville's *Caelica* and the Calvinist Self', *Studies in English Literature*, 32 (1992), 35–57. Argues that Greville recasts Petrarchan forms to present a Calvinist narrative of self-definition.
Larson, Charles, *Fulke Greville* (Boston: Twayne, 1980). Introduction to Greville's life and writings.
Powell, Neil (ed.), *Fulke Greville: Selected Poems* (Manchester: Carcanet, 1990). Misleadingly titled student edition of *Caelica* with little annotation.
Rebholz, Ronald A., *The Life of Fulke Greville, First Lord Brooke* (Oxford: Clarendon Press, 1971). Detailed historical biography.
Rees, Joan, *Fulke Greville, Lord Brooke, 1554–1628* (London: Routledge, 1971). Discusses Greville's life and works.
Steggle, Matthew, 'Greville's Buxton Poem: A Text and Commentary', *Sidney Journal*, 20:1 (2002), 55–68. On an early Greville poem not included in Bullough's edition.
Waswo, Richard, *The Fatal Mirror: Themes and Techniques in the Poetry of Fulke Greville* (Charlottesville: University Press of Virginia, 1972). Excellent for both intellectual background and detailed close study of Greville's works.
Wilkes, G. A. (ed.), *The Remains, Being Poems of Monarchy and Religion* (London: Oxford University Press, 1965). Critical edition of two of Greville's verse treatises.

Sir Robert Sidney

Croft, P. J. (ed.), *The Poems of Robert Sidney* (Oxford: Clarendon Press, 1984). Definitive scholarly edition.
Hay, Millicent V., *The Life of Robert Sidney* (Washington, DC: Folger Shakespeare Library, 1984). Scholarly biography.
Warkentin, Germaine, 'Robert Sidney's "Darcke Offrings": The Making of a Late Tudor Manuscript *Canzoniere*', *Spenser Studies*, 12 (1992), 37–73. Examines the composition of Robert's manuscript collection.

Lady Mary Wroth

Cavanagh, Sheila T., *Cherished Torment: The Emotional Geography of Lady Mary Wroth's Urania* (Pittsburgh: Duquesne University Press, 2001). Study of the intellectual and philosophical debates Wroth grapples with in her prose romance.
Miller, Naomi J., *Changing the Subject: Mary Wroth and Figurations of Gender in Early Modern England* (Lexington: University Press of Kentucky, 1996). Critical study discussing Wroth in relation to authorial strategies used by early modern women writers.
——, and Gary Waller (eds), *Reading Lady Mary Wroth: Representing*

Alternatives in Early Modern England (Knoxville: University of Tennessee Press, 1991). Essay collection.
Roberts, Josephine A. (ed.), *The Poems of Lady Mary Wroth* (Baton Rouge: Louisiana State University Press, 1983). Detailed scholarly edition.
—— (ed.), *The First Part of The Countess of Montgomery's Urania* (Binghamton, NY: Medieval and Renaissance Texts and Studies, 1995).
——, et al. (ed.), *The Second Part of The Countess of Montgomery's Urania* (Tempe, AZ: ACMRS, 1999).
Waller, Gary, *The Sidney Family Romance: Mary Wroth, William Herbert and the Early Modern Construction of Gender* (Detroit: Wayne State University Press, 1993). Theoretically engaged study of the sexual and textual relations between Wroth and her cousin William Herbert.

BACKGROUND READING

Amadis de Gaule, Translated by Anthony Munday, ed. Helen Moore (Aldershot: Ashgate, 2004). Early seventeenth-century translation of one of Sidney's sources for his pastoral romance.
Attridge, Derek, *Well-Weighed Syllables: Elizabethan Verse in Classical Metres* (Cambridge: Cambridge University Press, 1974). Still the standard work on early modern quantitative verse.
Bates, Catherine, *The Rhetoric of Courtship in Elizabethan Language and Literature* (Cambridge: Cambridge University Press, 1992). On the relationship between the amorous and political aspects of 'courting'. Includes a discussion of Sidney's works.
Bruno, Giordano, *The Ash Wednesday Supper*, ed. and trans. E. A. Gosselin and L. S. Lerner (Toronto: University of Toronto Press, 1977; repr. 1995). Translation of Bruno's *La Cena de la Ceneri*, an account of Sidney and Greville's discourse with the Italian philosopher on Ash Wednesday 1584.
Heliodorus, *Aethiopian Story*, trans. Walter Lamb, ed. J. R. Morgan (London: Everyman, 1997).
Javitch, Daniel, *Poetry and Courtliness in Elizabethan Poetry* (Princeton: Princeton University Press, 1978). Explores the links between the language and forms of poetry and courtship, making great use of Puttenham's treatise.
Montemayor, Jorge de, *A Critical Edition of Yong's Translation of George of Montemayor's Diana and Gil Polo's Enamoured Diana*, ed. Judith M. Kennedy (Oxford: Clarendon Press, 1968). Modern edition of the 1598 translation.
Rivers, Isabel, *Classical and Christian Ideas in English Renaissance Poetry*

(2nd edn, London: Routledge, 1994). Superb reference guide to the religious, mythological and philosophical background to early modern literature.

Russell, D. A., and M. Winterbottom (eds), *Classical Literary Criticism* (Oxford: Oxford University Press, 1989). Includes works by Aristotle and Horace, and selections from Plato.

Sannazaro, Jacopo, *Arcadia*, trans. R. Nash (Detroit: Wayne State University Press, 1966).

Spingarn, J. E., *A History of Literary Criticism in the Renaissance* (2nd edn, Westport, CT: Greenwood Press, 1976). Useful contextualization of the *Defence*.

Tasso, Torquato, *Discourses on the Heroic Poem*, trans. M. Cavalchini and I. Samuel (Oxford: Clarendon Press, 1973). Illuminating contemporary treatise on heroic poetry.

Zim, Rivkah, *English Metrical Psalms: Poetry as Praise and Prayer, 1535–1601* (Cambridge: Cambridge University Press, 1987). Authoritative introduction to the form.

INTERNET RESOURCES

Early English Books Online. Invaluable subscription-based resource providing online facsimiles (and an increasing number of searchable text versions) of all books published in England between 1473 and 1700. <eebo.chadwyck.com/home>

The Literary Encyclopedia. Reliable scholarly reference database. <www.litencyc.com>

Luminarium. Reference resource providing biography, criticism, images and selected texts for a wide range of medieval and early modern writers. Online essays are of mixed quality. <www.luminarium.org/renlit>

Penshurst Place. Website for visitors to the Sidney family seat at Penshurst, Kent. <www.penshurstplace.com>

Renascence Editions. High-quality online editions of works by Sidney and the Sidney circle (among a host of others). <darkwing.uoregon.edu/~rbear/ren.htm>

The Sidney Homepage. Site run through Cambridge University English faculty. The best online starting point for Sidney studies, includes searchable texts, biographies, further bibliography and links to the *Sidney Journal* (formerly *Sidney Newsletter*), a print-based journal published twice a year. Also has extensive material on Robert and Mary Sidney and Lady Mary Wroth. <www.english.cam.ac.uk/sidney>

Index

Aesop, 29
Alexander the Great, 76
Alexander, Sir William, 73
Amadis de Gaule, 20, 46
Anjou, Francis, Duc d', 15, 33–4
Anne, Queen of Denmark, 99–100
Ariosto, Ludovico, 21, 46, 52
    Orlando Furioso, 21, 46
Aristotle, 6, 40–2, 47, 66
    Poetics, 41
    Rhetoric, 6
Ascham, Roger, 21, 37
Ashton, Thomas, 3

Bacon, Francis, 45
Barnfield, Richard, 62
Bartas, Guillaume du, 62, 76, 78
    La semaine, 76
Bates, Catherine, 5
Benjamin, Walter, 10
Bèze, Théodore de, 75, 87
Book of Homilies, 81
Breton, Nicholas, 82–3
Bryskett, Lodowick, 18, 77
Buchanan, George, 47
Bunyan, John, 31
Byrd, William, 62

Calvin, John, 44–5, 53, 60, 74, 92, 95
    Institutes, 44
Campion, Thomas, 62

Cary, Elizabeth, 90
    Tragedy of Mariam, The, 90
Casimir, Prince Johann, 15, 60
Castiglione, Baldassare, 1, 6–7, 61, 83
    Book of the Courtier, The, 1, 6
Cecil, Sir Robert, 78
Cecil, Sir William, Lord Burghley, 2
Charles I, 74
    Eikon Basilike, 74
Charles IX, King of France, 3
Chaucer, Geoffrey, 20, 23, 40
    Troilus and Criseyde, 20
Churchill, Winston, 77
Churchyard, Thomas, 48, 77
    Brief Epitaph, 77
    Musicall Consort, A, 48
Cicero, 38, 40
Clifford, Margaret, Countess of Cumberland, 94

Daniel, Samuel, 62, 82, 86–7, 89–90
    Cleopatra, 86–7, 90
    Philotas, 86
Dante, 52
David, King of Israel, 41, 87–9
Davis, Joel, 79
Davison, Francis, 12
    Poetical Rapsody, A, 12
Day, John, 79
    Ile of Gulls, 79

119

INDEX

Denny, Sir Edward, 48
Denny, Edward, Baron Waltham, 102
Devereux, Penelope, 3, 29, 58–9
Devereux, Robert, second Earl of Essex, 76, 93
Devereux, Walter, first Earl of Essex, 2–4
Diana, Princess of Wales, 77
Donatus, 23
Donne, John, 6, 25, 89
  'Ecstasy, The', 25
  'Satyre 5', 6
  'Upon the translation of the Psalms', 89
Dowland, Robert, 62
Drummond, William, 21
Dudley, Ambrose, Earl of Warwick, 2
Dudley, John, Duke of Northumberland, 2
Dudley, Robert, Earl of Leicester, 2–3, 9, 12–15, 33, 59, 75–6, 93
Dyer, Sir Edward, 7–8, 10, 12, 18, 22, 29, 60, 76, 97

Edward VI, 1–2
Elizabeth (movie), 33
Elizabeth I, 1–5, 7–10, 12–16, 18, 29, 32, 35, 38, 59, 73, 76–8, 89–90, 92–3, 98
Essex, Earls of, *see* Devereux, Robert and Walter,
Evans, Maurice, 51, 66, 74

Fielding, Henry, 26
Florio, John, 78
Fraunce, Abraham, 6, 24–5, 82
  Arcadian Rhetorike, The, 24–5
Garnier, Robert, 85–6
  Cornelie, 86
  Marc Antoine, 85
Gascoigne, George, 9, 20, 29, 37
  'Notes of Instruction', 37

Posies, 37
Gentili, Scipio, 16
Glapthorne, Henry, 67
Golding, Arthur, 76
  The Trewnesse of the Christian Religion, 76
Gosson, Stephen, 37–8, 44, 47
  School of Abuse, The, 37
Greenblatt, Stephen, 6–7
Greene, Robert, 8
Greville, Fulke, 3, 8, 10 , 12, 18–19, 29, 31, 43, 60, 62–3, 76, 78–97
  Alaham, 86, 93–4
  Caelica, 29, 60, 62, 91–2, 95–6
  Inquisition upon Fame and Honour, An, 10
  Letter to an Honourable Lady, A, 94
  Life of Sidney, The, (A Dedication to Sir Philip Sidney), 31, 43, 76, 78, 94
  Mustapha, 86, 93–4
  Treatie of Humane Learning, A, 95
  Treatise of Monarchy, A, 94–5
  Treatise of Religion, A, 95
Grey, Lady Jane, 2
Gwinne, Matthew, 78

Harington, Sir John, 21, 58, 85
Harvey, Gabriel, 1, 13, 22, 91
Hayward, John, 78
Heliodorus, 20
  Aethiopica, 20
Henry VIII, 52
Herbert, Lord Edward of Cherbury, 76
Herbert, Henry, second Earl of Pembroke, 10, 12, 82, 89
Herbert, Mary, *see* Sidney, Mary,
Herbert, William, third Earl of Pembroke, 77, 100, 102
Holinshed, Raphael, 15–16, 78

INDEX

Chronicles, 15–16, 78
Homer, 40, 71
  Odyssey, The, 71
Horace, 40, 42
  Art of Poetry, The, 42
Hoskins, John, 6, 68
  Directions for Speech and Style, 68
Howard, Henry, Earl of Surrey, 36, 52, 54

Jonson, Ben, 21, 79, 89, 99–100
  Alchemist, The, 99–100
  Forest, The, 99
  'To Penshurst', 99

Kyd, Thomas, 86

Landino, Cristoforo, 40
Languet, Hubert, 3, 29–30, 42
Lant, Thomas, 77
Lanyer, Aemilia, 90
  Salve Deus Rex Judaeorum, 90
Lee, Sir Henry, 10, 73
Leicester, Earl of, see Dudley, Robert,
Leicester's Commonwealth, 75
Lewis, C.S., 36, 59
Lister, Sir Matthew, 90
Locke, Anne, 53
Lyly, John, 24
  Euphues, 24

Malory, Sir Thomas, 20–21, 26
  Morte Darthur, 20–21, 26
Marlowe, Christopher, 8
Marot, Clément, 75, 87
Marotti, Arthur, 59, 62, 92
Mary I, 1–2
Mary of Nassau, 2
Mary, Queen of Scots, 73, 77
Medici, Catherine de', 33, 73
Melissus, Paulus, 18
Milton, John, 45, 74

Eikonoklastes, 74
Minturno, Antonio, 40
Mirror for Magistrates, The, 36
Moffet, Thomas, 77, 82
  Nobilis, 77
Molyneux, Edmund, 15, 18
Montemayor, Jorge de, 20
  Diana, 20
Montgomery, Countess of, see Vere, Susan de,
More, Sir Thomas, 43, 81
  Utopia, 43
Morley, Thomas, 62
Mornay, Philippe de, 62, 76, 83–5
  De la vérité, 76
  Discourse of Life and Death, The, 83–5
Mucedorus, 79
Mulcaster, Richard, 37

Nashe, Thomas, 1, 8, 49, 53
  Preface to Astrophil, 49, 53
Newman, Thomas, 49, 62
Norton, Thomas, 47
  Gorboduc, 47

Olney, Henry, 48
Ovid, 29
Oxford, Earl of, see Vere, Edward de,

Parker, Patricia, 68
Peele, George, 10
  Polyhymnia, 10
Pembroke, Countess of, see Sidney, Mary,
Pembroke, Earls of, see Herbert, Henry and William,
Petrarch, Francis, 7, 29, 51–3, 55–62, 71, 84–5, 88, 91, 96–8, 100–03
  Rime Sparse, 51–3, 55
  Trionfi, 84–5, 103
Philip II, King of Spain, 1–2

Plato, 5, 25, 34, 37, 39–42, 44–6,
    50, 61
  Republic, The, 34, 37, 42, 44, 46
Plutarch, 76
Ponsonby, William, 48
Pugliano, John Pietro, 36, 38
Puttenham, George, 6, 47, 52, 91
  Arte of English Poesie, The, 6, 52

Quarles, Francis, 67
Quintilian, 38–9

Raleigh, Sir Walter, 4–5, 8, 48, 77
Ramus, Petrus, 48
Rich, Lord Robert, 58
Rogers, Daniel, 18
Rudolf II, Holy Roman Emperor, 4
Russell, Lucy, Countess of Bedford, 85

Sackville, Thomas, 47
  Gorboduc, 47
Sanford, Hugh, 79
Sannazaro, Jacopo, 20, 28
  Arcadia, 20, 28
Scaliger, Julius Caesar, 41
  Poetices libri septem, 41
Shakespeare, William, 13, 47, 50,
    56, 59, 62, 67, 79, 86, 89
  Antony and Cleopatra, 86
  Hamlet, 53
  Henry V, 47
  Love's Labours Lost, 13
  King Lear, 67
  Sonnets, 56, 59, 62
  Venus and Adonis, 50
Shirley, James, 79
  Arcadia, 79
Sidney, Barbara, née Gamage, 98
Sidney, Elizabeth, Countess of Rutland, 99
Sidney, Sir Henry, 1–2, 4, 73, 83
Sidney, Lady Mary, née Dudley, 2, 73, 83
Sidney, Mary, Countess of Pembroke, 10, 12, 18–19, 26,
    29, 34–5, 62, 70, 75, 78–90, 97, 99
  Antonius, 85–6, 90, 94
  'Dialogue between two shepherds, Thenot and Piers, A', 12, 89
  Discourse of Life and Death, The, 83–5
  'Even now that Care', 89
  Psalm translations, 75, 87–9
  'To the Angell spirit', 89
  Triumph of Death, The, 84–5
Sidney, Sir Philip,
  Accession day tilt songs, 9–10, 16, 28
  Astrophil and Stella, 3, 24, 28–9, 49–62, 77, 84, 86, 88, 91, 97–8
  Certain Sonnets, 10, 28, 49
  De la vérité translation, 76
  Defence of Leicester, The, 75
  Defence of Poesy, The, (*An Apology for Poetry*), 6, 8, 11, 18, 20, 22, 24, 31, 35–48, 57, 60–61, 67, 70, 75, 86, 95
  'Dialogue between two shepherds, A', 10–12, 89
  'Discourse on Irish Affairs', 4
  'Disprayse of Courtly Life', 12
  Four Foster Children of Desire, The, 10, 15, 34, 59
  'La Cuisse Rompue', 76
  Lady of May, The, 12–15, 32, 38
  Lamon's Tale, 63
  La semaine translation, 76, 78
  Letter to the Queen, 33
  New Arcadia, The, 10, 20–21, 32–5, 38, 40, 44, 47, 59, 62–76, 78–9, 83, 86, 100–02
  Old Arcadia, The, 5, 10, 15–16, 18–35, 38–40, 44, 46, 48–9,

59, 63, 65–7, 77–8, 83, 86, 90, 100–02
Psalm translations, 62, 75–6, 78, 87, 89
Rhetoric translation, 6
'Seven Wonders of England, The', 83
Sidney, Sir Robert, 1, 3, 10, 19, 48, 83, 93, 96–9
Spenser, Edmund, 4, 9, 12, 22, 25, 31, 33, 48, 62, 73, 77, 79, 87, 91, 100
  Amoretti, 62, 91
  Astrophel, 12, 77
  Colin Clouts Come Home Againe, 12, 77
  'Dolefull Lay of Clorinda, The', 77
  Faerie Queene, The, 9, 48, 100
  Fowre Hymnes, 25
  Mother Hubberds Tale, 33
  Shepheardes Calender, The, 77
Sterne, Lawrence, 26
Stow, John, 78
  Annales, 78
Surrey, Earl of, *see* Howard, Henry,

Tasso, Torquato, 21, 40
Temple, William, 48
  Analysis, 48
Terence, 23
Throckmorton, Elizabeth, 8

Tottel, Richard, 36, 52
  Miscellany, 36, 52

Valla, Giorgio, 41
Vere, Edward de, seventeenth Earl of Oxford, 7–8, 29, 33
Vere, Susan de, Countess of Montgomery, 100
Vindiciae contra tyrannos, 30
Virgil, 11, 78
  Aeneid, The, 78
Vives, Juan Luis, 81

Waller, Gary, 60
Walsingham, Frances, 3, 93
Walsingham, Sir Francis, 3, 78
Watson, Thomas, 53
  Hekatompathia, 53
Whetstone, George, 77
Whyte, Rowland, 10
William of Orange, 2
Willis, Richard, 40
  De re poetica disputatio, 40
Wilson, Sir Thomas, 6, 38
  Arte of Rhetoric, The, 6, 38
Worden, Blair, 32
Wroth, Lady Mary, 62, 90, 99–103
  Love's Victory, 90, 103
  Pamphilia to Amphilanthus, 62, 101
  Urania, 90, 99–103
Wroth, Sir Robert, 99–100
Wyatt, Sir Thomas, 36, 52

www.ingramcontent.com/pod-product-compliance
Lightning Source LLC
Chambersburg PA
CBHW030143240426
43672CB00005B/251